Penguin  Classics

PLATO
PHAEDRUS
& LETTERS VII AND VIII

D0046944

THE PENGUIN CLASSICS

FOUNDER EDITOR (1944–64): E. V. RIEU

EDITORS:

Robert Baldick (1964–72) *Betty Radice*

PLATO (*c.* 427–347 B.C.) stands with Socrates and Aristotle as one of the shapers of the whole intellectual tradition of the West. He came from a family that had long played a prominent part in Athenian politics, and it would have been natural for him to follow the same course. He declined to do so however, disgusted by the violence and corruption of Athenian political life, and sickened especially by the execution in 399 of his friend and teacher, Socrates. Inspired by Socrates' inquiries into the nature of ethical standards, Plato sought a cure for the ills of society not in politics but in philosophy, and arrived at his fundamental and lasting conviction that those ills would never cease until philosophers became rulers or rulers philosophers. At an uncertain date in the early fourth century B.C. he founded the Academy in Athens, the first permanent institution devoted to philosophical research and teaching, and the prototype of all western universities. He travelled extensively, notably in Sicily as political adviser to Dionysius II, ruler of Syracuse.

Plato wrote over twenty philosophical dialogues, and there are also extant under his name thirteen letters, whose genuineness is keenly disputed. His literary activity extended over perhaps half a century: few other writers have exploited so effectively the grace and precision, the flexibility and power, of Greek prose.

WALTER HAMILTON has been Master of Magdalene College, Cambridge, since 1967. He was born in 1908 and was a Scholar of Trinity College, Cambridge, where he gained first class honours in both parts of the classical Tripos. He was a Fellow of Trinity College and a University Lecturer at Cambridge, and taught at Eton before becoming Headmaster of Westminster School (1950–57) and of Rugby School (1957–66). He has translated Plato's *Symposium* and his *Gorgias* for the Penguin Classics.

PLATO

PHAEDRUS

AND

THE SEVENTH AND
EIGHTH LETTERS

*

TRANSLATED WITH
INTRODUCTIONS BY
WALTER HAMILTON

PENGUIN BOOKS

Penguin Books Ltd, Harmondsworth, Middlesex, England
Penguin Books Australia Ltd, Ringwood, Victoria, Australia

—

This translation first published 1973

—

Made and printed in Great Britain by
Hazell Watson & Viney Ltd,
Aylesbury, Bucks
Set in Monotype Garamond

CONTENTS

*

INTRODUCTION

*

I

THE *Phaedrus* is chiefly valued by lovers of the classics for its idyllic setting and its magnificent myth. It touches, however, on so many of the main themes of Platonic philosophy that it is unusually difficult to grasp its structure as a whole. Even in later antiquity it was debated whether it was primarily concerned with love or with rhetoric, or even with more general concepts such as the soul or the good or the beautiful. Before discussing its structure it will be well to consider it in relation to other dialogues, and to formulate some conclusion about its place in the general development of Plato's thought.

Diogenes Laertius (third century A.D.) reports a tradition which has found defenders even in modern times, that the *Phaedrus* is the earliest of all Plato's works. No time need be spent in demonstrating the absurdity of this belief. Both style and content show conclusively that it is a work of Plato's maturity, and there are strong grounds for supposing that it is later than both the *Republic* and the *Symposium*. References to some of the arguments on this point will be found in the notes. Here it may suffice to say that the famous comparison of the soul to a charioteer with two horses involves the same psychological scheme that is propounded with considerable emphasis upon its novelty in *Republic* IV, and that it is, to say the least, improbable that Plato could have made Phaedrus declare in the *Symposium* that 'nobody to this day has had the courage to praise Love in such terms as he deserves' if he had already composed the great speech in praise of love which Socrates delivers to Phaedrus himself in the present dialogue. It is widely accepted that the *Phaedrus* is probably the latest of the great central group of dialogues to which the *Symposium* and the *Republic* also belong (a date of about 370 B.C. may be very tentatively suggested), and it cannot be disputed that these two dialogues shed light on much in the *Phaedrus* which would otherwise be obscure.

To return now to the question of structure. The dialogue begins with the reading by Phaedrus of a speech purporting to be by the celebrated Attic orator Lysias which maintains a paradoxical thesis about love. Socrates finds this profoundly unsatisfactory and offers to provide an alternative speech on the same theme. When he has done so he is on the point of leaving Phaedrus, but is prevented from doing so by his 'divine sign', an inward monitor which convinces him that he, no less than Lysias, has been guilty of blasphemy against love by discussing it on the merely physical level, and that he must purge his contempt by a treatment of the subject on altogether different lines. This second speech of Socrates begins with a severely dialectical proof of the eternal existence of the soul, but goes on to describe its nature and destiny in what Plato calls a myth or 'probable story', a method which he reserves for topics which cannot be treated by rigorous argument, and which he employs here to give in apocalyptic form a vision of the heaven of truth and beauty from which the soul has fallen. With this is combined an allegorical treatment of the passion of love which finds its counterpart in the speech of Diotima to Socrates in the *Symposium*. Here, as there, Plato finds in the emotion of love directed aright the key to the whole quest of the philosopher; truth is to be attained by a partnership of two like-minded people, based perhaps in the first instance on physical attraction, but soon leaving this behind in the common pursuit of the beauty not of this world which is ultimately to be identified with the Form of Good, and which gives meaning and coherence to the whole of reality.[1] This is the love against which Lysias and Socrates have blasphemed by restricting the term to physical passion, and to which reparation has now been made not in cold-blooded argument but in

1. As in the *Symposium* the love which forms the basis of discussion is homosexual love. For a discussion of this and of the philosophic quest which it can inspire cf. Hamilton, *Symposium*, Penguin Classics, pp. 12–26.

the highest and most inspired poetry of which even Plato is capable.

At this point comes an abrupt change of tone and apparently of subject which can hardly fail to give the impression of anticlimax. The conversation returns to Lysias, and the rest of the dialogue is occupied with a discussion of rhetoric based on the three speeches which have been delivered, and involving criticism in considerable detail of contemporary rhetorical practice. How is this to be related to what we have so far heard? Are the speeches simply illustrations of sound and vicious principles of rhetoric, and is their subject irrelevant to the future course of the conversation? It is difficult to suppose that Plato, who makes Socrates announce to Phaedrus the principle that 'any composition ought to have its own organic shape, like a living being'[1] has committed a gross violation of his own principle in the very dialogue in which it is enunciated.

The solution of the problem lies in a clearer understanding of the view of the nature of rhetoric which Plato is putting forward in the *Phaedrus*. In the *Gorgias*, a considerably earlier dialogue, philosophy and rhetoric are treated as mutually incompatible and exclusive; the former is the search for truth, the latter merely an 'unscientific knack'. The *Phaedrus* gives a more sophisticated treatment of this antithesis. Plato's views have not fundamentally changed; rhetoric as practised by his contemporaries is still an 'unscientific knack', but rhetoric in itself is no longer condemned root and branch; there can be such a thing as a scientific or philosophic rhetoric or art of persuasion, and the main purpose of the *Phaedrus* is to establish the true principles of that rhetoric. They must be based on knowledge of truth; but truth, as we have already learnt from the *Symposium* and as Socrates' second speech has made clear to us, is only to be attained through the inspiration of love. Socrates' speech, therefore, is not merely an example of philosophic rhetoric in action; it is at the same time an exposition of the experience

1. 264C.

on which that rhetoric, like any other philosophic activity, must be founded. We are led back to the common subject of all three speeches, and we see that it is no accident that that subject is love.

The dialogue ends with a condemnation of writing as a means of communicating knowledge which cannot fail to ring oddly in the ears of a modern reader. Yet here too is to be found the same underlying thought. In origin dialectic, as its name implies, is a process in which truth is elicited by conversation; it is the method adopted by the historical Socrates, who left nothing in writing, and it remained the method employed by Plato in the Academy. Truth emerges from the direct action of one mind on another, when both are kindled by the inspiration of love;[1] it is to be found 'only in words spoken by way of instruction or, to use a truer phrase, written on the soul of the hearer to enable him to learn about the right, the beautiful and the good'.[2] In comparison written communication is a poor second-best, a kind of pastime with which the philosopher may amuse himself in his less serious moments, at its highest no more than an aid to recollection of truth already discovered.

Are we then to conclude that Plato seriously regarded his own writings as being only of secondary importance? In view of their volume and the care which he clearly lavished on them that would probably be going too far. Perhaps, however, a hint can be found in the *Phaedrus* itself which would account for the severity of Plato's depreciation of writing at the time when it was composed. If the main purpose of the dialogue is to establish the principles of a genuine rhetoric, it has to be admitted that the scope and elaboration of Socrates' great second speech are out of proportion. In view of the fact that the speech marks one of the highest points in Plato's achievement as artist and poet we can hardly regret this, but it has undoubtedly contributed to the uncertainty which has pre-

1. cf. the Seventh Letter 344A, where it is also emphasized that the most important philosophical truths cannot be put into written form.
2. *Phaedrus* 278A.

vailed about the interpretation of the *Phaedrus* as a whole. It may be that it is because he is conscious of this disproportion, conscious that in Socrates' speech the poet in him has got the better of the philosopher, that he subsequently refers to the speech as a 'pastime' (*paidia*),[1] the same word, it is to be noted, which he uses to characterize written composition as a whole.[2] And it may be not irrelevant in this connection to add that throughout the dialogue we are reminded again and again that Socrates' speech is the product of a type of inspiration quite unusual with him and symbolized by the unusual nature of the setting and of the powers which haunt it.

The *Phaedrus* has sometimes been described as Plato's farewell to literature. To assert this is to ignore the myth of Atlantis which introduces the *Timaeus*, but, leaving that aside, it is true that in the works which can be confidently dated after the *Phaedrus* the strictly philosophical element predominates more and more, and that Plato is much less concerned to charm as well as to instruct his readers.

2

The *Phaedrus* is a conversation in direct speech between only two persons, Socrates and Phaedrus. Socrates is the mature Socrates of the *Republic* and *Symposium*, the exponent of the developed metaphysical doctrine to be found in those dialogues. He is, however, Socrates with a difference; a new and unexpected element is added to his character which Plato is at pains to emphasize. In the *Phaedrus*, and nowhere else, he is represented as sensitive to the influence of the powers of external nature, to whose inspiration he professes to owe the exalted poetic tone of his second speech. This serves to diminish our sense of the incongruousness of such a speech in the mouth of the Socrates whom we know, just as in the *Symposium* a similar effect is achieved by ascribing to the

1. 265C.
2. 276D.

fictitious wise woman Diotima the culminating account of the nature and function of love.

Phaedrus is a historical character, though we know little of him apart from what Plato tells us. He is mentioned in the *Protagoras* as a member of the group gathered round the sophist Hippias, and depicted in much greater detail in the *Symposium*, where he originates the idea that the company should entertain itself by speeches in praise of love and himself delivers the first in the series, a poor affair which treats love only in its physical sense, and which is quite consistent with the admiration which he expresses in the present dialogue for the equally uninspired speech of Lysias. He is, in fact, a person of shallow and uncritical enthusiasms, the eager but superficial follower of any new fashion in culture, though at the end he seems to be genuinely converted to Socrates' view.

The dramatic date of the *Phaedrus* cannot be precisely determined like that of the *Symposium*, but must lie between 411 and 404 B.C. Lysias, who is treated as the acknowledged representative of contemporary rhetoric, returned to Athens after a long residence at Thurii in 411, and his brother Polemarchus, who is mentioned as still living, perished at the hands of the Thirty Tyrants in 404. Such a date involves a slight but unimportant difficulty about the age of Phaedrus. The dramatic date of the *Protagoras* cannot be set later than about 432, and Phaedrus must therefore have been born at latest by about 450. Yet in the *Phaedrus* he is addressed by Socrates as 'young man' and even on one occasion as 'boy'. It suits Plato's dramatic purpose and his conception of Phaedrus' character to lay stress upon his immaturity, and it is of little consequence that this involves him in a slight anachronism.

3

Lysias, the apparent author of the speech on which the dialogue is founded, plays so important a part in the *Phaedrus* that some account of him is needed. Though one of the most famous of the Attic orators he was not himself an Athenian. His father was Cephalus, a Syracusan and the owner of a shield factory at Piraeus. Lysias spent much of his early manhood at Thurii in southern Italy, where he is said to have studied rhetoric under Tisias; on his return to Athens in 411 he may have taught rhetoric and acquired by the composition of showpieces the reputation which he enjoys in the *Phaedrus*, but it seems improbable that he became a professional writer of speeches for the law courts till after the ruin of his family in 404 and the restoration of the democracy in 403. From that time onwards he was a prolific writer of speeches for litigants – professional advocates did not plead themselves in Athenian courts – and of his great output some thirty speeches have been preserved. They have always been regarded as specimens of Attic style at its purest and most limpid.[1]

It has been much debated whether the speech read by Phaedrus to Socrates is a genuine production of Lysias or an invention by Plato. The question cannot be settled by a comparison of its style with those of Lysias' acknowledged speeches, most of which are in any case of quite different type, since Plato could no doubt have produced an excellent imitation of Lysias' style had he wished to do so. It must therefore be argued on more general grounds.

On the one side it is urged that we have no other example in Plato of the incorporation verbatim of a passage of anything like this length by another author; no one supposes that the myth in the *Protagoras* or the earlier speeches in the *Symposium* are the actual productions of the speakers in whose mouth they are placed, though they provide excellent illustrations of Plato's mastery and enjoyment of the art of pastiche. On this view of the matter Lysias' speech is designed by Plato to illustrate the general characteristics of the kind of rhetoric of which he disapproves, and the name and perhaps something

1. For a specimen of Lysias' speeches which also tells us much about his adventures in 404/3 cf. his speech against Eratosthenes in Saunders, A. N. W., *Greek Political Oratory*, Penguin Classics, 1970.

of the style of Lysias are added simply to enhance its verisimilitude. If this seems to us a very odd proceeding we have to remember that the standards of Plato's day were very different from our own, so different that in the *Phaedo*, for example, it is possible for him to make Socrates at the point of death base his belief in the immortality of the soul on a theory which cannot have been held by the historical Socrates. A further consideration is that it is improbable that there should have been available to Plato among the works of Lysias a speech so peculiarly appropriate to his purpose in content as well as in style.

There is, however, much force in the contrary contention that Plato's criticism of contemporary rhetoric would be vitiated if the speech on which it is exercised were a fictitious composition of his own, however cleverly it incorporated the rhetorical traits of its age. Further it must be noted that Plato is at great pains to emphasize that the speech is *read* by Phaedrus from a copy which he has with him – Socrates is made explicitly to reject Phaedrus' offer to give the gist of it from memory – and that the criticism directed at it is not only of its general tone but of its particular defects as a rhetorical exercise. And, finally, for what it is worth, it must be added that the speech was accepted as a genuine production of Lysias in later antiquity.

No definite answer to the question is attainable; every reader must form his own conclusion. To the present translator the arguments in favour of authenticity seem on the whole slightly the more compelling.

4

At the end of the dialogue (279A) Lysias is compared unfavourably with a second famous rhetorician, Isocrates, in whom Socrates professes to detect potentialities of a greatly superior kind. Isocrates, a slightly older contemporary of Plato, is a writer of an altogether different type from Lysias.

He had abandoned at an early stage in his life the composition of speeches for the law courts, and had established himself as a writer of political pamphlets in the form of speeches[1] and as the head of a highly influential school, in which rhetoric was made the vehicle of higher education, and which may be regarded as in some sense a rival to Plato's Academy. Although Isocrates was critical of the kind of rhetorical training which consists in the inculcation of ready-made rules, and claimed for his own system the name of philosophy, his educational methods and aims were in strong contrast to those of the Academy with its emphasis on the attainment of objective truth, and in several places he speaks contemptuously of what he regards as the unpractical and useless pursuits of his contemporary. Plato's attitude to Isocrates is less easy to determine. There is an ancient tradition that their personal relations were friendly, but Plato can hardly have viewed with more than strongly qualified approval the activities of an educator whose system was avowedly based on opinion rather than knowledge. What then is meant when Isocrates is described by Phaedrus as Socrates' 'friend', and Socrates says of Isocrates that he is not 'devoid of a certain love of wisdom (*philosophia*)', and that he would not be surprised if as he grew older 'he becomes dissatisfied with his present pursuits and is driven by some divine inspiration to greater things'?

By the time of the composition of the *Phaedrus* Isocrates' course was set, and it was surely vain to hope for any fundamental change in his outlook. For this reason the famous compliment has been treated by some as ironical, or even as a taunt. But Isocrates has not been previously mentioned in the dialogue at all, and, seeing that he was unquestionably the best-known rhetorician of his age, it is not unreasonable to suppose that Plato places him in a different category from the

---

1. For examples of Isocrates' work as a publicist cf. his *Panegyricus* and *Philip* in Saunders, op. cit., pp. 101ff, and for some account of the contrast with Plato ibid., pp. 13ff.

other rhetoricians whom he is criticizing.[1] He may well have recognized in Isocrates qualities more 'philosophical' than any displayed by Lysias; and if we ask what possible grounds he could have had for expecting a change of heart in him, it can be answered that the Plato who was prepared to embark on the project of converting Dionysius II to philosophy need not have entirely despaired even of the middle-aged Isocrates. Moreover, if a philosophic rhetoric of the kind which Plato is seeking to establish were ever to come into being, this could only be brought about by winning over Isocrates, the most famous living teacher of rhetoric. It seems likely therefore that Cicero[2] is right when he speaks of the compliment as a genuine expression of Plato's opinion.

A more far-reaching suggestion, which involves the whole interpretation of the *Phaedrus*, has been made by Professor H. L. Hudson-Williams.[3] It is that Socrates' first speech is meant to exemplify the type of rhetoric practised by Isocrates, unquestionably superior to that of Lysias, but falling far short of the philosophic rhetoric of which Socrates' second speech is to provide a supreme instance. Such a view is not at first sight unattractive; it links the three speeches in a clear structure and it provides an obvious motive for the reference to Isocrates as Socrates' friend. Nevertheless, it seems unlikely that if this were Plato's purpose he would not have made it much plainer. It is of course true that any overt mention of Isocrates as the established head of a school would be an anachronism in the mouth of Socrates, but it is Lysias who remains to the end the representative of the unsound rhetoric which Plato is criticizing. From this criticism, as has been suggested, Plato seems to regard Isocrates as being, at any rate to some extent, immune.

1. Critics have detected various allusions to Isocrates in the latter part of the *Phaedrus* (cf. de Vries, *A Commentary on the Phaedrus*, p. 16), but these, even if they were more certainly established than they are, could hardly be said to constitute an attack on Isocrates.

2. *Orator* 13.41.

3. *Three Systems of Education* (an inaugural lecture delivered at King's College, Newcastle), 1954.

5

It has already been suggested that the *Phaedrus* will be most easily intelligible to the reader who comes to it after the *Symposium* and the *Republic*. The bearing of the great myth, in particular, can hardly be grasped without some acquaintance with the Theory of Forms, which constitutes Plato's distinctive contribution to metaphysics. The essential feature of this theory is that reality is to be found only in a world of eternal and unchanging Forms, of which the shifting phenomena of the sensible world are imperfect imitations or copies, and to which the latter owe such half-reality as they possess. The Forms are in fact universals given the status of independent and absolute entities; although the precise content of Plato's real world is difficult to establish, it is broadly true that there exists a Form for every class of things which can be embraced under a common name, beauty, for example, or triangle or horse. The Forms, arranged in a hierarchy at the head of which stands the Form of Good,[1] constitute the only true objects of knowledge; as the myth tells us, they can be contemplated by the soul before its incarnation, and the business of the philosopher is to make use of the 'reminders' of them furnished by the sensible world as a starting-point in his pilgrimage back from the changing world of sense and opinion to the eternal world of reality and truth. This pilgrimage, best undertaken, Plato believes, by two like-minded people in collaboration and culminating in a mystical vision of reality which is incommunicable,[2] involves both intellect and emotion: it is described on its intellectual side in the central books of the *Republic*; the *Symposium* represents the same quest as inspired by love, and to this the *Phaedrus* myth is in many ways complementary. It is most important to realize that, in

1. For the ultimate coincidence of the Forms of Good and Beauty cf. Hamilton, *Symposium*, pp. 20ff.

2. cf. Plato's Seventh Letter 344 (p. 140 below).

spite of the highly poetical colouring of the myth, the ideas which underlie it, the existence of the Forms themselves and the process by which knowledge of them can be recaptured, are for Plato not matters of speculation but of dialectically established truth.

6

This translation, like that of the two Platonic letters which follow, attempts no more than to introduce to English readers an admittedly difficult and comparatively little-read dialogue, in which there are many obscurities and unsolved problems. A few books for further reading are listed in the Bibliography. The translator is indebted to Mr A. N. W. Saunders for many helpful criticisms of the translation.

THE PHAEDRUS

PRELUDE

*

Socrates meets Phaedrus, who has spent the morning listening to a speech by Lysias, and in order to hear it reproduced consents to accompany him on a walk in the country outside Athens. The scene on the banks of the Ilissus is described in vivid detail, and it is emphasized that Socrates is in unfamiliar surroundings, and that such an excursion is quite contrary to his usual habits.

SOCRATES: Where have you come from, my dear Phaedrus, 227
and where are you going?

PHAEDRUS: I have been with Lysias, the son of Cephalus,
Socrates, and I am going for a walk outside the walls after
a long session with him that has lasted since early morning.
Our common friend, Acumenus,[1] says that a country walk
is more refreshing than a stroll in the city squares; that is
why I am going in this direction.

SOCRATES: Acumenus is quite right, my friend. So Lysias
was in the city, was he?

PHAEDRUS: Yes, he was visiting Epicrates, in the house you
see there near the temple of Olympian Zeus, the house that
used to belong to Morychus.

SOCRATES: What were you doing there? Lysias was entertaining you with his eloquence, I suppose?

PHAEDRUS: You shall hear, if you can spare the time to go
with me.

SOCRATES: Spare the time! Don't you realize that to me an
account of what passed between you and Lysias is, to use
Pindar's phrase, 'a matter which takes precedence even
over business'?[2]

PHAEDRUS: Come along then.

1. A well-known physician, father of Eryximachus, one of the speakers
in the *Symposium*.
2. Pindar, *Isthmians* 1.2.

SOCRATES: Your story, please.

PHAEDRUS: Well, Socrates, what I have to tell is very much in your line, for the subject on which we were engaged was love – after a fashion. Lysias has written a speech designed to win the favour of a handsome boy for someone who is not in love with him. That is the clever thing about it; he makes out that an admirer who is not in love is to be preferred to one who is.

SOCRATES: Noble fellow! I only wish he would prove that a poor lover is preferable to a rich, and an old lover to a young, and deal in the same way with all the other disadvantages under which I, like most of us, labour. Then his speeches would be delightful indeed and a blessing to the public. Really, I have conceived such a passionate desire to hear your account that even if you prolong your walk as far as the walls of Megara and then, in the manner of Herodicus,[1] turn straight back, I won't be left behind.

PHAEDRUS: Come, come, my good Socrates. Do you suppose that an amateur like me can adequately reproduce what it took Lysias, the best writer living, so much time and study to compose? Of course not. Yet I'd rather be able to do that than come into a fortune.

SOCRATES: My dear Phaedrus, I know my Phaedrus as well as I know my own name. And that being so I'm convinced that he wasn't content with a single hearing of Lysias' speech but made him repeat it a number of times, and that Lysias willingly complied. But even that didn't satisfy Phaedrus, and in the end he took the manuscript and went over his favourite passages by himself. Finally, exhausted by sitting at this occupation since early morning, he went out for a walk with the whole speech, I could swear, firmly in his head, unless it was excessively long. His motive in going outside the walls was to be able to declaim it aloud. Imagine his delight when he met a man whose passion for such speeches amounts to a disease; now he would have

228

1. Another physician and a native of Megara, who particularly recommended long walks.

some one to share his enthusiasm, so he asked him to go along with him. But when the speech-lover asked him to repeat the speech he grew coy and affected reluctance, though in fact he meant to force it on his companion in the end, whether he wanted it or not. So now, Phaedrus, beg him to do without further delay what he is eventually going to do in any case.

PHAEDRUS: Well, the only course for me is to repeat the speech as best I can, since you clearly won't let me go till I have given you some sort of satisfaction.

SOCRATES: You need be in no doubt about that.

PHAEDRUS: Well, this is what I will do. I didn't learn the speech by heart, Socrates, I assure you, but I will summarize point by point from the beginning the argument of almost all that Lysias said about the superiority of the man not in love to the man in love.

SOCRATES: Yes, but before you begin on that, dear heart, just let me see what it is you are holding in your left hand under your cloak; I strongly suspect it is the actual speech. If I am right you can make up your mind to this, that, much as I love you, I have no intention of letting you use me to rehearse on when I might have Lysias himself. Come on, show me.

PHAEDRUS: Enough of that. You've dashed my hope of using you to practise on, Socrates. Where would you like us to sit down and read?

SOCRATES: Let us turn aside here along the Ilissus. Then we can sit down in peace wherever we feel inclined. 229

PHAEDRUS: It's lucky I came out without shoes. You, of course, never wear them. Our easiest way is to get our feet wet and walk in the stream. Pleasant enough too, especially at this hour and time of year.

SOCRATES: Go ahead, and look out for a place for us to sit.

PHAEDRUS: Do you see that very tall plane tree?

SOCRATES: What about it?

PHAEDRUS: There is shade there and a gentle breeze, and grass to sit on, or lie, if we prefer.

SOCRATES: Lead on then.

PHAEDRUS: Tell me, Socrates, isn't there a story that Boreas abducted Oreithyia[1] from somewhere here on the banks of the Ilissus?

SOCRATES: So they say.

PHAEDRUS: Was it here, do you think? The water is delightfully fresh and clear, just the place for girls to play.

SOCRATES: No, it was some quarter of a mile downstream, where one crosses to the temple of Agra; an altar to Boreas marks the spot, I believe.

PHAEDRUS: I haven't noticed it. But seriously, Socrates, do you believe this legend?

SOCRATES: The pundits reject it, so if I rejected it too I should be in good company. In that case I should rationalize the legend by explaining that the north wind blew Oreithyia down the neighbouring rocks when she was playing with Pharmaceia, and that her dying in this way was the origin of the legend that she was abducted by Boreas. (Or else she fell from the Areopagus, for according to one version the abduction took place from the Areopagus, not from here.) But though I find such explanations very attractive, Phaedrus, they are too ingenious and laboured, it seems to me, and I don't altogether envy the man who devotes himself to this sort of work, if only because, when he has finished with Oreithyia, he must go on to put the Hippocentaurs[2] into proper shape and after them the Chimaera.[3] In fact he finds himself overwhelmed by a host of Gorgons

1. Oreithyia is the daughter of Erechtheus, one of the legendary kings of Athens. Pharmaceia, her playmate, is the nymph of a spring, perhaps with medicinal properties, near the Ilissus. Boreas is the north wind. The allegorical interpretation of myths was fashionable among some sophists. Plato makes Socrates reject it on the ground that a philosopher should concern himself with more important topics.

2. Creatures half man, half horse.

3. A mythical monster, with the head of a lion, the tail of a snake, and the body of a goat. It was killed by Bellerophon with the help of the winged horse Pegasus. Pegasus himself sprang from the body of the Gorgon, Medusa, the sight of whom turned the beholder to stone.

and Pegasuses and other such monsters, whose numbers create no less a problem than their grotesqueness, and a sceptic who proposes to force each one of them into a plausible shape with the aid of a sort of rough ingenuity will need a great deal of leisure. Now I have no time for such work, and the reason is, my friend, that I've not yet succeeded in obeying the Delphic injunction to 'know myself',[1] and it seems to me absurd to consider problems about other beings while I am still in ignorance about my own nature. So I let these things alone and acquiesce in the popular attitude towards them; as I've already said I make myself rather than them the object of my investigations, and I try to discover whether I am a more complicated and puffed-up sort of animal than Typho[2] or whether I am a gentler and simpler creature, endowed by heaven with a nature altogether less typhonic. But while we are talking, my friend, haven't we reached the tree that you were making for?

PHAEDRUS: This is the very place.

SOCRATES: It is indeed a lovely spot for a rest. This plane is very tall and spreading, and the agnus-castus splendidly high and shady, in full bloom too, filling the neighbourhood with the finest possible fragrance. And the spring which runs under the plane; how beautifully cool its water is to the feet. The figures and other offerings show that the place is sacred to Achelous[3] and some of the nymphs. See too how wonderfully delicate and sweet the air is, throbbing in response to the shrill chorus of the cicadas – the very voice of summer. But the most exquisite thing of all is the way

1. The inscription 'Know thyself' upon the temple of Apollo at Delphi expresses the essence of the philosophy of Socrates, who turned philosophy away from the study of external nature to that of man as a moral being.

2. Typho is the father of the winds, a monster with a hundred heads. By a play on words Plato connects the name with the noun *tuphos*, vanity or arrogance, and its negative adjective *atuphos*, here translated 'less typhonic'.

3. The river god *par excellence*.

the grass slopes gently upward to provide perfect comfort
for the head as one lies at length. Really, my dear Phaedrus, a
visitor could not possibly have found a better guide than you.

PHAEDRUS: What a very strange person you are, Socrates.
So far from being like a native, you resemble, in your own
phrase, a visitor being shown the sights by a guide. This
comes of your never going abroad beyond the frontiers of
Attica or even, as far as I can see, outside the actual walls of
the city.

SOCRATES: Forgive me, my dear friend. I am, you see, a
lover of learning. Now the people in the city have something to teach me, but the fields and trees won't teach me
anything. All the same you have found a way to charm me
into making an expedition. Men lead hungry animals by
waving a branch or some vegetable before their noses, and
it looks as if you will lead me all over Attica and anywhere
else you please in the same way by waving the leaves of a
speech in front of me. For the moment, however, having
got as far as this, I mean to lie down; so choose whatever
position you think will be most comfortable for the
purpose and read to me.

THE SPEECH OF LYSIAS

*The speech of Lysias, whether authentic or not, is a rhetorical
exercise, which advances the paradox that a suitor whose aim is
merely the gratification of physical desire is to be preferred to one who
is genuinely in love. Love is not defined; it is taken for granted that it is
an aberration or form of madness, and the frankly materialistic
arguments of which the speech is composed are based on this assumption. The speech is bad both in style and content, but it contains a
thought on which Socrates will later build, the thought that the lover is
not a man in his sober senses. The peculiar appropriateness of the
speech in this respect to Plato's purpose is perhaps the strongest
argument against its being an actual work of Lysias.*

PHAEDRUS: Listen then.

'You know my situation, and you have heard how I think that it will be to our advantage for this to happen. I beg you not to reject my suit because I am not in love with you. Lovers repent the kindnesses they have shown when their passion abates, but to men not in love there never comes a time for such regret. They behave as generously as their means allow, not under constraint but with their eyes open, after deliberate calculation of their own interests. Again, lovers bring into account not only the kindnesses they have shown but also the losses they have incurred in their own affairs on account of their passion, and when they add to this the trouble they have undergone they consider that the debt they owe to their favourites has been discharged long ago. Those who are not in love, on the other hand, cannot use as a pretext for coolness the excuse that love has made them neglect their own interests, or put into the reckoning the hardships they have endured, or hold the loved one responsible for their having quarrelled with their families; and since they are relieved from all these disadvantages nothing remains for them but to do cheerfully whatever they think will give their partners pleasure. Again, if lovers deserve to be made much of because they declare that whoever they are in love with has a supreme claim on their friendship, and because they are prepared to say and do what will incur the hostility of others in order to please their beloved, then, if their professions are genuine, the conclusion plainly follows that they will value any new love in future more than the old, and even be ready to inflict an injury on the old love if the new love requires it. And how can it be sensible in a matter of such importance to trust oneself to a man suffering from a disorder of a kind that no experienced person would even attempt to cure? Lovers themselves admit that they are mad, not sane, and that they know that they are not in their right mind but cannot help themselves. How then can one expect that designs formed in such a condition will meet with their approval when they come to their senses? Besides, if you choose the best from among your lovers, you will have few to choose from, whereas, if you look for the man who suits you best in the world at large, you will have a wide field of choice, and so a much better chance of finding in it the man who is worthy of your friendship.

'Now, if you are afraid that public opinion will condemn you when men hear of your love affairs, reflect that the lover, believing that others will envy his good fortune as much as he values it himself, is likely in a state of elation and gratified pride to publish generally the fact that his efforts have not gone unrewarded, whereas the man not in love, having better control of himself, will probably subordinate reputation to what is in fact the best course. Again, numbers of people will inevitably see or hear of the lover persistently dogging the footsteps of his beloved, so that whenever they are observed talking to one another it will be supposed that they are together because they have just gratified or are about to gratify their passion; those not in love incur no blame at all for keeping company, since people realize that one man may have occasion to talk to another because he is his friend or because the conversation gives him pleasure for some other reason. Then again, you may be alarmed by the reflection that friendships are easily broken, and that if that happens the greater part of the harm will fall on you, who have sacrificed your dearest possession, whereas a quarrel in other circumstances is a misfortune shared by both parties equally. In that case you have all the more reason to be afraid of those who are in love with you; they can be hurt in such a variety of ways and are apt to interpret anything as a personal slight. That is why they do not like their favourites to consort with anyone else; they may be outbidden by the rich or found inferior in intelligence to the educated, and similarly they are on their guard against the possessor of any other advantage. If they succeed in getting you to break with such people, you are left without a friend in the world; if you consult your own interests, and show more sense than your lovers you will quarrel with *them*.

Those not in love, on the other hand, who owe their success in their suit to their own good qualities, so far from being jealous of your associates, will hate those who shun your society; they will feel slighted themselves by such behaviour and positively obliged by those who cultivate you. So such an affair as I suggest is much more likely to win you friends than enemies.

'Besides, with most of your lovers physical attraction will have preceded any knowledge of your character or acquaintance with your circumstances; it must therefore be uncertain whether they will want to remain your friends when their passion has cooled. But those not in love, who were friends before they formed a liaison, are in no danger of finding their friendship diminished as a result of the satisfaction they have enjoyed; on the contrary, the recollection of it will be a pledge of further satisfaction to come. Moreover, you have a better chance of improving yourself by yielding to me than by yielding to a lover. Lovers approve words and actions that are far from excellent, partly because they are afraid of getting themselves disliked and partly because their passion impairs their judgement. One of love's feats is this: it makes lovers, when they are out of luck, treat as grievances things which cause no pain to ordinary men; when they are fortunate it compels them to bestow praise on things which do not deserve even the name of pleasant. So those who are in love are far more to be pitied than admired by the objects of their passion. But if you yield to *my* suit you will find that I, being my own master and not under the dominion of love, shall in all our dealings have an eye more to future advantage than to present pleasure. I shall not allow trifling causes to engender violent hostility; on the contrary, I shall be slow to exhibit a small degree of anger even on serious provocation; offence given involuntarily I shall overlook, and intentional slights I shall endeavour to avert; this is the way to lay the foundation of lasting affection. If you are possessed by the notion that firm friendship is impossible unless one is in

love, let me remind you that in that case we should have
little regard for our sons, or our fathers and mothers, nor
should we have made loyal friends whose friendship is
based not on passion but on associations of quite a different
kind.

'Again, if you hold that we should show favour to those
who press their suit most strongly, we must extend this
principle further and show kindness not to the most
deserving but to the most necessitous, whose gratitude will
be proportionate to the severity of the hardships from which
we relieve them. Not only so, but when we give a private
party our guests should be not our friends but beggars in
need of a good meal; they are the people who will love us
for it and attach themselves to us and come about our doors;
they will be the best pleased and the most grateful, and will
call down countless blessings on the head of their host.
Nevertheless, the truth may be that it is not the most
insistent that you should favour, but those best able to
make a return; not lovers merely, but those who show
themselves worthy of what they ask; not those who will
simply enjoy your youthful charms, but those who will share
their possessions with you when you are older; not those who
will boast of their success to others, but those whom modesty
will keep completely silent; not those who are keen on you
just for the moment, but those who will remain your firm
friends for life; not those who will look for an excuse to
break with you when their passion wanes, but those who
will show themselves good men and true when your good
looks have vanished. Remember what I have said, and bear
in mind too that lovers are liable to be reproached by their
friends for the sorry state they are in, whereas those who are
not in love are never blamed by any of their relatives on the
ground that they are neglecting their true interests.

'Perhaps you may ask whether I advise you to yield
indiscriminately to anyone who is not in love. No more, I
answer, than the lover would urge you to show such a
disposition to all who *are* in love; such behaviour would

lessen your value in the eyes of your admirer, and make it less possible for you to avoid the notice of the world. A liaison of this kind ought to be free from all ill effects, and an advantage to both parties. I think that I have said enough, but if I have omitted any point that you would like me to touch on, by all means ask me.'

INTERLUDE

Socrates refuses to take Lysias' speech seriously, but, to humour Phaedrus, professes, perhaps ironically, to find some merit in its style. He offers jokingly to make a better speech himself on the same theme, and is ultimately cajoled by Phaedrus into making good his offer. He does so with reluctance, and this reluctance, though ostensibly due to modesty, really arises from dislike of the thesis which he has to treat. In fact, he confines himself to arguing that it is wrong to yield to a lover of the sensual type described by Lysias; he refuses to complement this by an argument in favour of the non-lover.

PHAEDRUS: Well, what do you think of the speech, Socrates? Isn't it a wonderful piece of work, especially the diction?

SOCRATES: More than wonderful, my friend, divine; it quite took my breath away. It is you who are responsible for this effect on me, Phaedrus. I concentrated on you and saw how what you were reading put you in a glow; so, believing that you know more about these things than I do, I followed your example and joined in the ecstasy, you inspired man.

PHAEDRUS: Do you think that this is a laughing matter?

SOCRATES: Why, don't you think I'm serious?

PHAEDRUS: Don't talk like that, Socrates. But tell me seriously, in the name of friendship, do you think that there is another man in Greece who could produce a grander and fuller discourse on this subject than what we have heard?

SOCRATES: Well, must our approval of the speech extend to its matter, or may we confine ourselves to admiring the clarity and shapeliness and precision with which every phrase is turned? If the former, it is you who must take the responsibility. I am such an idiot that I let it pass me by and attended only to the style; the matter I didn't suppose that even Lysias himself could think satisfactory. I submit to your better judgement, Phaedrus, but it seems to me that he has said the same things two or three times over, either because he could not find sufficient matter to produce variety on a single topic, or perhaps from sheer lack of interest in the subject. The speech struck me as a piece of youthful exhibitionism; an attempt to demonstrate how he could say the same thing in two different ways, each as good as the other.

PHAEDRUS: Nonsense, Socrates. If the speech has one merit above all others, it is that no single aspect of the subject worth mentioning has been omitted; no one could improve on it either in fullness or quality.

SOCRATES: Here I can go along with you no further. If I give way, to please you, wise men and women of old who have spoken and written on the subject will prove me wrong.

PHAEDRUS: Who are they? And where have you heard it better treated?

SOCRATES: I can't tell you off-hand, but certainly by some-one, either lovely Sappho or wise Anacreon or some prose writers. I am sure of this because my own heart is full and I have a feeling that I could compose a different speech not inferior to this. Now I am far too well aware of my own ignorance to suppose that any of these ideas can be my own. The explanation must be that I have been filled from some external source, like a jar from a spring, but I am such a fool that I have forgotten how or from whom.

PHAEDRUS: My good friend, you never said a better word. Never mind how or from whom – don't tell me even if I ask you – just do what you've said; provide me with another speech better and equally full, avoiding the arguments already used. I promise I'll do like the nine archons, and set

PHAEDRUS

up at Delphi a life-size image in gold of you as well as of myself.[1]

SOCRATES: You are a dear fellow, Phaedrus, genuine gold all through, if you suppose me to mean that Lysias has completely missed the mark, and that it is possible to compose a second entirely different speech. That could hardly be true even of the feeblest writer. Take the thesis of his speech to begin with; if one is arguing that the non-lover is to be preferred to the lover, how can one avoid taking the obvious line of praising the good sense of the former and censuring the folly of the latter? No, we must not find fault with commonplaces of that sort; their use must be allowed and treated with forbearance, though it is only by their skilful arrangement and not by their originality that they can earn praise; whereas less obvious and more recondite ideas are to be commended for their novelty as well as for their neat use.

236

PHAEDRUS: I concede your point, which seems very reasonable. I will let you take for granted that the lover is in a less healthy state than the non-lover, and if you can produce a speech which is otherwise different from Lysias' and more copious and convincing as well, you shall stand in wrought gold at Olympia beside the offering of the Cypselids.[2]

SOCRATES: Are you taking me seriously, Phaedrus, because by way of teasing you I made an attack on your favourite? Do you think that I shall make a serious attempt to outdo the clever Lysias by something more subtle?

PHAEDRUS: If it comes to that, my friend, you have laid yourself open to the same treatment as you gave me. Unless we are to indulge in an exchange of the sort of vulgar repartee that occurs in comedies, you had better deliver

1. Aristotle, *Constitution of Athens* 7.1., says that the archons of Athens swore to dedicate a golden statue if they transgressed the law. He does not say that it was to be at Delphi or that it was to be life-size; the latter point is perhaps added by Phaedrus by way of hyperbole.

2. The Cypselids are the descendants of Cypselus, the father of Periander, the celebrated tyrant of Corinth. Strabo says that their offering was an image of Zeus.

your speech to the best of your ability. Don't drive me to
say: 'Socrates, I know Socrates as well as I know my own
name; he was longing to speak but he was coy.' Take it
from me that we are not going to leave this spot till you
have uttered what you said you had in mind. We are alone
and I am younger and stronger than you, so 'mark my
words'[1] and don't compel me to use force to get what you
may as well supply without reluctance.

SOCRATES: But, my good Phaedrus, it would be ludicrous
for a layman like myself to extemporize on a subject which
has been already treated by a good writer.

PHAEDRUS: You know the situation, so stop playing with
me. Anyhow, I fancy that I can say something which will
make you speak.

SOCRATES: Then don't say it.

PHAEDRUS: I certainly shall. Here it is and it takes the form
of an oath. I swear to you by – what god shall I invoke? Or
shall it be this plane tree? Yes; I swear by this tree that
unless you deliver your speech in its actual presence I will
never give you sight or word of another speech by anybody.

SOCRATES: Oh, you wretch, what a splendid device for
making a man who loves speeches do what you want.

PHAEDRUS: Then why go on shuffling?

SOCRATES: Since you have taken this oath, I won't. I can't
cut myself off from that kind of entertainment.

237 PHAEDRUS: Speak on then.

SOCRATES: Shall I tell you what I'll do?

PHAEDRUS: What?

SOCRATES: I'll speak with my face covered. In that way I
shall get through the speech most quickly, and I shan't be
put out by catching your eye and feeling ashamed.

PHAEDRUS: You may do what you like if you'll only begin.

1. An adaptation of a well-known phrase of Pindar.

SOCRATES' FIRST SPEECH

Socrates begins by declaring that any discussion must begin by defining the topic to be discussed; accordingly love, still the merely sensual love taken for granted by Lysias, is defined as an irrational desire for the enjoyment of physical beauty. The lover is a person in whom this irrational desire has got the better of rational judgement, and it is shown that in this condition his influence on a boy's mental, physical and material welfare cannot fail to be injurious. Finally, the speech describes the disagreeable results of such an association for the beloved, first, while his admirer is in love with him, and second, when he has returned to his sober senses.

The orderly arrangement of the speech is in strong contrast with the incoherence and repetitiveness of that of Lysias. Its superiority, however, is not confined to its form. The speaker, unlike Lysias, has in view the real welfare of the imaginary boy he is addressing; the sensual lover will prevent him from pursuing 'divine philosophy', and will 'do harm above all to his spiritual development, than which nothing is or ever will be more precious in the sight of God or man'. This explains the curious point made by Socrates at the beginning of the speech that the speaker is a 'subtle person' who is really in love with the boy though he pretends not to be so. He is, in fact, a lover of the kind whom Plato would approve, the type which Socrates himself represents in his relations with Alcibiades in the Symposium, *where he totally rejects Alcibiades' physical advances. Nothing in the speech conflicts in any fundamental way with Plato's own views; it has already been noted that Socrates will refuse to argue in favour of yielding to the non-lover, and, if he later declares this speech to be blasphemous, that is not because its substance is in itself to be rejected, but because it is confined to a discussion of a completely inadequate and unworthy type of love, the 'left-hand love' which he will distinguish from 'right-hand' love in the great speech which is to follow.*

For the view that this speech is meant to be representative of the rhetoric of Isocrates cf. Introduction, Section 4.

SOCRATES: Come then, shrill Muses, whether it be to the character of your song or to the tuneful race of Ligurians

that ye owe your name of shrill [*ligeiai*],[1] help me in the tale
which this fine gentleman is forcing me to tell, in order that
his friend, whom he already thinks so brilliant, may seem to
him hereafter even more brilliant than before.

Once upon a time there was a boy, or rather a lad, who
was exceedingly handsome. Among his many admirers
there was one subtle person, no less in love than the rest,
who had, however, persuaded the lad that he was not in
love with him. And once in the course of his suit he was
trying to convince him that a man not in love has a better
claim to be favoured than a lover. His argument was as
follows:

In every discussion, my dear boy, there is one and only
one way of beginning if one is to come to a sound conclusion; that is to know what it is that one is discussing; otherwise one is bound entirely to miss the mark. Now most
people are unaware that they are ignorant of the essential
nature of their subject, whatever it may be. Believing that
they know it, they do not begin their discussion by agreeing
about the use of terms, with the natural result that as they
proceed they fall into self-contradictions and misunder-
standings. Do not let us make the mistake for which we
find fault with others. The subject that we are discussing is
whether the friendship of a lover or of a non-lover is
preferable. Let us begin then by agreeing upon a definition
of the nature and power of love, and keep this before our
eyes to refer to as we debate whether love does good or
harm.

Love is a kind of desire – everyone will admit that – but
we know that one does not have to be in love to desire what
is beautiful. How then are we to distinguish between a
lover and his opposite? We must realize that in each one of
us there are two ruling and impelling principles whose
guidance we follow, a desire for pleasure, which is innate,
and an acquired conviction which causes us to aim at

1. A fanciful etymology of a kind of which Plato is fond, and of which
there are other examples in this speech and elsewhere in the dialogue.

excellence. These two principles are sometimes in agreement within us and sometimes at variance; at one moment the first and at another the second prevails. The conviction which impels us towards excellence is rational, and the power by which it masters us we call self-control; the desire which drags us towards pleasure is irrational, and when it gets the upper hand in us its dominion is called excess. Excess has many categories and takes many forms and goes by a variety of names. Whichever of these forms is most in evidence confers upon its possessor its own peculiar name, an acquisition which is far from being honourable or valuable. If, for example, the desire which prevails over sound reason and all the other desires is concerned with food, it is called gluttony, and its possessor will receive the corresponding name of glutton; if on the other hand the desire which gains absolute sway and leads its possessor down its own particular path is desire for drink, we do not need to be told what he will be called; and similarly with the kindred desires and their names: whichever of them happens at any moment to be dominant, we are left in no doubt of the appropriate name. The conclusion to which all this is leading is obvious, but for the sake of clarity it is better to be quite explicit. When the irrational desire that prevails over the conviction which aims at right is directed at the pleasure derived from beauty, and in the case of physical beauty powerfully reinforced by the appetites which are akin to it, so that it emerges victorious, it takes its name from the very power with which it is endowed and is called *eros* or passionate love.[1]

Tell me, my dear Phaedrus, do you think, as I do, that I am inspired?

PHAEDRUS: Undoubtedly you have been carried away by a quite unusual flow of eloquence, Socrates.

SOCRATES: Be quiet then and listen. This spot seems full of spirits, so do not be surprised if, as my speech goes on, the

1. A play on the words rhome (power) and eros.

nymphs take possession of me. In fact, what I am uttering now is almost lyrical.

PHAEDRUS: Very true.

SOCRATES: *You* are responsible for this. But listen to what remains; perhaps the madness that is coming upon me may yet be averted. We must leave that to God; our business is to resume the argument addressed to the lad.

Well then, my good fellow, we have defined in words the subject of our discussion. With this in mind let us go on to the further question what good or harm is likely to result from the lover and the non-lover respectively to the person who yields to them.

The man who is under the sway of desire and a slave to pleasure will inevitably try to derive the greatest pleasure possible from the object of his passion. Now a man in a morbid state finds pleasure in complete absence of opposition, and detests any appearance of superiority or equality in his darling; he will always do his best to keep him in a state of inferiority and subservience. Seeing therefore that an ignoramus is inferior to a wise man, a coward to a hero, a poor speaker to a man of eloquence, a slow mind to a quick wit, a lover will inevitably be delighted if he finds these and a number of other mental defects part of the natural endowment of his beloved, or will do his best to foster them if they are in the course of being acquired; otherwise he must lose the prospect of immediate enjoyment. Moreover, he will of course be jealous, and by keeping his favourite from the kind of society most likely to help him to become a man he will do him great harm. The worst form that this harm can take is deprivation of what would make him most intelligent, that is to say of divine philosophy; a lover is bound to keep him away from this for fear of incurring his contempt, and generally speaking to do everything in his power to ensure that he shall be totally ignorant and totally dependent upon the lover, a state in which he will give the greatest pleasure to his admirer and inflict the greatest injury upon himself. So, as

239

far as his mind is concerned, he cannot have a less desirable protector or companion than a man who is in love with him.

Next consider what kind of physical condition the man who is forced to pursue pleasure rather than good will hope to find or will encourage in anyone whom he gets into his power. The person we shall see him running after will be soft rather than tough, the product of a breeding in chequered shade rather than clear sunshine, a stranger to manly toil and honest sweat, accustomed to luxurious and effeminate living, supplying his natural deficiency of complexion by the use of cosmetics, and indulging in all the other practices that go with these characteristics. We know what they are; there is no need to pursue the matter further; we can sum up in a single phrase and pass on. In war or any other great emergency a physical condition such as I have described inspires as much confidence in the enemy as fear in one's own side and even in one's lovers themselves.

So much is obvious and we can proceed to the next point – how will the society and protection of a lover affect one's material circumstances for good or harm? Everyone knows, and the lover above all, that he would like his favourite to be devoid of the dearest and kindest and most perfect belongings than a man can have; he would be quite happy for him to be without father or mother or kindred or friends, because their disapproval is likely to prevent him from deriving the highest enjoyment from the 240 liaison. As for property in cash or in any other form, the existence of this will in his opinion make the pursuit more difficult, and the pursued less easy to handle even when he is in the toils. The lover, then, will inevitably grudge his favourite the possession of wealth and be glad when he loses it. In addition, he will naturally pray that his beloved should remain wifeless, childless, and homeless for as long as possible, because he wants to enjoy the sweets of possession for the longest possible time.

Many other things which are bad in themselves nevertheless by some dispensation of providence have a momentary pleasure attached to them. A toady, for instance, is a dreadful animal and does much harm, yet the ready wit which nature has implanted in him is a source of pleasure. The trade of a prostitute is mischievous and one may condemn such creatures and their activities, yet the enjoyment that they afford is very sweet while it lasts. But the companionship of a lover, besides being injurious, is in the highest degree disagreeable to the object of his passion. Like to like, as the old proverb says; equals in age have the same pleasures, and this similarity begets friendship; but the society even of one's contemporaries palls in the end. Besides, every kind of constraint is felt to be a burden, and that is precisely what a lover imposes on his darling in addition to their discrepancy of age. He is old and his companion is young, yet he never leaves his side day or night if he can help it; he is driven on by an irresistible itch to the pleasures which are constantly to be found in seeing, hearing, and touching his beloved, in fact in every sensation which makes him conscious of his presence; no wonder then that he takes delight in close attendance on him. But what compensating pleasures are there for the other party to prevent a companionship of such length ending in utter distaste? Before his eyes is a man older than himself and no longer in his first youth, with all the defects that go with advancing years, defects which it is disagreeable even to hear of, far more to come into physical contact with under the pressure of a necessity which never relaxes. Worse still, he is the object of jealous vigilance at all times and in all company; he has to listen to unseasonable and excessive praise of himself, or else to reproaches which are hard to bear even when the lover is sober, but which when he is drunk are disgraceful as well as intolerable, owing to the disgusting and unreserved freedom with which they are uttered.

While he is in love the lover is a tedious nuisance, but when his passion cools you can place no reliance on him for the future, in spite of all the promises which he mixed with his oaths and entreaties in order to maintain, through the expectation of benefits to come, a precarious hold upon an intimacy which even then the beloved found irksome. When the time comes to pay his debts he is under the sway of a new influence; rational self-control has replaced the madness of love; he is a different man and has forgotten his darling. So when the latter treats him as if he were still the same, and reminds him of what he did and said, and asks him to requite the favours he has received, he is ashamed to say that he has changed, but does not know how to fulfil the oaths and promises which he made when he was the slave of irrational passion. Now that he has come to his senses and regained his self-control he has no wish to behave as he did in the past and thus to relapse into his former condition. So the sometime lover has no choice but to escape his creditor by flight; the other side of the coin has come uppermost now, and it is his turn to run away, while his former favourite is forced to pursue him with angry reproaches, all because he did not realize at the start that it is far better to yield to a non-lover who is in his sober senses than to a lover who from the very nature of things is bound to be out of his mind. The alternative is to put oneself in the power of a man who is faithless, morose, jealous, and disagreeable, who will do harm to one's estate, harm to one's physical health, and harm above all to one's spiritual development, than which nothing is or ever will be more precious in the sight of God and man. Take this to heart then, my lad, and learn the lesson that there is no kindness in the friendship of a lover; its object is the satisfaction of an appetite, like the appetite for food. 'As wolves for lambs, so lovers lust for boys.'[1]

1. The last words constitute the end of an hexameter, which may explain Socrates' reference to epic a few lines below. The source of the quotation, if it is a quotation, is unknown.

INTERLUDE

Socrates, having delivered his speech, is about to go away when he is prevented by his 'divine sign'. He must make reparation for the blasphemy involved by his treatment of love as evil. His proposal to deliver a palinode or recantation is warmly welcomed by Phaedrus.

It is noticeable that love is here assumed to be a god, whereas in the Symposium *he is a daemon, a being intermediate between gods and men. This arises not from any real discrepancy in Plato's thought but from the different ways in which the subject is developed. In the* Symposium *Diotima's exposition is based on the premise that love is the consciousness of need for the beautiful and good, and this is symbolized by making love a link between the sensible world and the world of the Forms. This thought is found also in the myth of the* Phaedrus, *where it is love that prompts the efforts of the soul to recapture the vision of the ideal world, but Socrates begins his exposition by describing love as a form of madness or divine possession, and it is in keeping with this to treat love in the traditional way as a god.*

SOCRATES: I told you how it would be, Phaedrus; you shan't hear another word from me. Make no mistake about it; my speech is over.

PHAEDRUS: But I thought you were only half way, and I was expecting you to balance what you have said already by describing the advantages to be derived from yielding to the man who is not in love. Why are you stopping at this point, Socrates?

SOCRATES: Haven't you noticed, bless you, that I have become not merely lyrical but actually epic, as if the former weren't bad enough? If I embark on a eulogy of the second type, what do you think will happen to me? These nymphs, to whose influence you meant to expose me all along, will drive me positively beside myself. Anyhow, there's no need for a long harangue: I've already said enough about both types; simply take the opposites of all the bad qualities I attributed to the first and confer them on 242   the second. My tale must meet with whatever fate it deserves; I shall cross the stream and go away, before you exercise some stronger compulsion on me.

PHAEDRUS: Don't go till the heat of the day is over, Socrates. Look, it's almost high noon already, and the sun is at its strongest. Let us stay here and discuss what we have heard and go away presently when it gets cool.

SOCRATES: Your passion for rhetoric, Phaedrus, is super-human, simply amazing. I really believe that no one in your life-time has been responsible for the production of more speeches than you, if we include besides those you deliver yourself those you somehow compel other people to deliver.[1] Simmias of Thebes[2] is an exception, but you beat the rest easily. And now it looks as if you have given occasion for yet another discourse from me.

PHAEDRUS: That's anything but a declaration of war. But tell me what you mean.

SOCRATES: Just as I was about to cross the stream, Phaedrus, I received the supernatural sign which sometimes comes to me[3] – every time it happens it restrains me from doing what I am about to do – and I seemed suddenly to hear a voice declaring that I had committed a sin and must not go away till I had expiated it. My powers of divination are only slight – in fact, I am like those readers who can just pick out their letters – but they are just sufficient for my own con-cerns. I see clearly now where my offence lies, for the soul itself is endowed with some power of divination. Even while I was speaking some time ago I felt a certain

---

1. In the *Symposium* Phaedrus is the author of the idea that those present should make speeches in praise of love.

2. Simmias, a Pythagorean, is one of the principal interlocutors of Socrates in the *Phaedo*. In the *Crito* he is said to have offered to find a sum sufficient to procure the liberation of Socrates.

3. Socrates' 'divine sign' is described in the *Apology* (31D) as an inner voice which came to him at intervals throughout his life, sometimes on quite trivial occasions, and forbade him to do what he was about to do. Its commands were always negative, never positive. To it he ascribes his abstention from political life (*Apology*, loc. cit., and *Republic* 496C).

uneasiness; in the words of Ibycus[1] I was afraid that I might be 'purchasing honour with men at the price of offending the gods'. Now I see where I went wrong.

PHAEDRUS: Where?

SOCRATES: Our speeches were dreadful, Phaedrus, dreadful, both the speech you brought with you and the speech you made me utter.

PHAEDRUS: In what way?

SOCRATES: They were silly and more than a little blasphemous. What could be worse than that?

PHAEDRUS: Nothing, if what you say is true.

SOCRATES: Well, don't you believe that Love is the son of Aphrodite and a god?

PHAEDRUS: So we are told.

SOCRATES: That is not how he was spoken of by Lysias, or in that speech of yours, which came out of my lips because you put a spell on them. If Love is a god, or at any rate a being with something divine about him, as he certainly is, he cannot be evil, but both our recent speeches represented him as being so. In that way both sinned against Love. What could be more exquisitely silly than for them to give themselves airs for the approval they could win by imposing on a few feeble mortals, when they did not contain a single sound or true idea? So then, my friend, I must purge my offence. For those who make mistakes in mythology there is an old remedy, which Stesichorus[2] was aware of, though Homer was not. When he lost his sight for speaking ill of Helen, Stesichorus, unlike Homer, was sagacious enough to understand the reason; he immediately composed the poem which begins:

1. A lyric poet from Rhegium in Southern Italy (early sixth century B.C.).

2. The story of Stesichorus being struck blind for speaking ill of Helen, and recovering his sight by a recantation, was a well-known legend. (The reference to Homer, also by legend blind, is a touch added by Plato.) But Stesichorus was an historical poet from Himera in Sicily (7th–6th centuries B.C.), and the lines quoted in the text do not suggest a separate poem. Perhaps the so-called 'palinode' was the second part of a poem in

> False is this tale. You never
> Went in a ship to sea,
> Nor saw the towers of Troy.

And as soon as he had finished what is called his palinode or recantation he recovered his sight. Now I propose to be even cleverer than our forebears; I mean to deliver a palinode to Love before I suffer any harm for the wrong I have done him, and I will deliver it with my head uncovered, not muffling myself up from bashfulness as I did before.

PHAEDRUS: Nothing you could have said would give me greater pleasure, Socrates.

SOCRATES: That, my good Phaedrus, is because you realize the irreverence of those two speeches, mine just now and the one you read from your manuscript. Anyone of good birth and breeding, in love with someone of like nature, or himself previously the object of love, who heard us saying that lovers conceive great hatreds for trivial reasons and behave jealously and injuriously to those they love, so far from agreeing with us in our aspersions on Love, would think that he was listening to men brought up among the scum of a sea-port, who had never seen what love between freeborn men was like.

PHAEDRUS: Perhaps you are right, Socrates.

SOCRATES: The thought of such a man makes me ashamed, and Love himself fills me with dread. So I am anxious to wash the brine out of my ears, so to speak, with the fresh water of some sound doctrine. And I advise Lysias too to lose no time in writing a speech to the effect that, other things being equal, one ought to favour a lover rather than a non-lover.

PHAEDRUS: You need have no fear about that. Once you

---

which Stesichorus, having first described Helen's flight to Troy with Paris on traditional lines, went on to another version in which Helen did not leave Sparta at all, but was represented at Troy by a phantom Helen (cf. *Republic* 586c). Euripides' *Helen* gives a story of similar type, though in this the real Helen is represented as being blown ashore in Egypt.

have spoken on the side of the lover I shall absolutely compel Lysias to write a speech on the same subject.[1]

SOCRATES: I feel sure of it, as long as you remain the man you are.

PHAEDRUS: Speak on then.

SOCRATES: Where is the lad I was addressing? I want him to hear this too, before for lack of it he falls into the error of yielding to the non-lover.

PHAEDRUS: He is always here at your elbow, whenever you need him.

SOCRATES' SECOND SPEECH
TYPES OF DIVINE MADNESS. THE IMMORTALITY OF SOUL.

Three acknowledged types of divine madness or possession are distinguished. To these is to be added a fourth type, that of the lover. First, however, the nature of soul must be demonstrated. Its immortality is deduced from its capacity of initiating motion; it is uncreated and indestructible.

SOCRATES: Well then, my handsome lad, you must realize that the previous speech was the work of Phaedrus, son of Pythocles, a man of Myrrhinus, whereas this which you are about to hear comes from Stesichorus, son of Euphemus, a native of Himera. This is how it must go. 'False is the tale' which says that because the lover is mad and the non-lover sane the non-lover should be given the preference when one might have a lover. If it were true without qualification that madness is an evil, that would be all very well, but in fact madness, provided it comes as the gift of heaven, is the channel by which we receive the greatest blessings. Take the prophetess at Delphi and the priestesses

---

1. Phaedrus takes it for granted that Lysias will be equally ready to support the reverse of the proposition which his speech maintained. It is this indifference to truth which provides the fundamental ground for Plato's condemnation of contemporary rhetoric and rhetoricians.

at Dodona,[1] for example, and consider all the benefits which individuals and states in Greece have received from them when they were in a state of frenzy, though their usefulness in their sober senses amounts to little or nothing. And if we were to include the Sibyl[2] and others who by the use of inspired divination have set many inquirers on the right track about the future, we should be telling at tedious length what everyone knows. But this at least is worth pointing out, that the men of old who gave things their names saw no disgrace or reproach in madness; otherwise they would not have connected with it the name of the noblest of all arts, the art of discerning the future, and called it the *manic* art. The fact that they did so shows that they looked upon madness as a fine thing, when it comes upon a man by divine dispensation, but their successors have bungled matters by the introduction of a T and produced the word *mantic*. Similarly, augury and the other methods by which men in their right minds inquire into the future, and through which they acquire insight and information by the exercise of purely human thought, were originally called *oiönoistic*,[3] but later generations by lengthening the O to make it sound impressive have brought it into connection with birds (*oi-ōnoi*), and called it *oiönistic*. So, according to the evidence provided by our ancestors, madness is a nobler thing than sober sense, in proportion as the name of the mantic art and the act it signifies are more perfect and held in higher esteem than the name and act of augury; madness comes from God, whereas sober sense is merely human.

1. Dodona in Epirus was the site of an oracular oak-tree sacred to Zeus. Its answers were given by the rustling of the leaves, and interpreted by the priests or priestesses.

2. A legendary prophetess, originally located in Asia Minor. In later times the number of Sibyls was multiplied, and various collections of oracular sayings were ascribed to them.

3. A word made up by Plato from the components *oiomai* (I think), *nous* (intelligence), and *historia* (inquiry). These etymologies can hardly be intended seriously.

In the next place, when ancient sins have given rise to severe maladies and troubles, which have afflicted the members of certain families, madness has appeared among them and by breaking forth into prophecy has brought relief by the appropriate means: by recourse, that is to say, to prayer and worship. It has discovered in rites of purification and initiation a way to make the sufferer well and to keep him well thereafter, and has provided for the man whose madness and possession were of the right type a way of escape from the evils that beset him.[1]

The third type of possession and madness is possession by the Muses. When this seizes upon a gentle and virgin soul it rouses it to inspired expression in lyric and other sorts of poetry, and glorifies countless deeds of the heroes of old for the instruction of posterity. But if a man comes to the door of poetry untouched by the madness of the Muses, believing that technique alone will make him a good poet, he and his sane compositions never reach perfection, but are utterly eclipsed by the performances of the inspired madman.

These are but some examples of the noble effect of heaven-sent madness. Intrinsically there is nothing in it to frighten us, and we must not allow ourselves to be alarmed and upset by those who say that the friendship of a man in his sober senses is preferable to that of one whose mind is disturbed. They will prove their case only if they can demonstrate in addition that love sent from heaven is not a blessing to lover and loved alike. It is for us to prove the opposite, and to show that this type of madness is the greatest benefit that heaven can confer on us. Our argument will carry conviction with the wise, though not with the merely clever. First of all we must form a true notion of the

1. The most celebrated instances of inherited curses are those which afflicted the descendants of Pelops (Agamemnon, Orestes) and Labdacus (Oedipus and his children). The idea that the frenzy which accompanies the curse may itself reveal a source of healing is well exemplified by Aeschylus in the *Oresteia*, where the madness brought upon Orestes by his guilt in murdering his mother leads him to seek purification and the restoration of his sanity from Apollo at Delphi.

nature of soul, divine and human, by observing it in both its passive and its active aspects. And the first step in our demonstration is this.

All soul is immortal;[1] for what is always in motion is immortal. But that which owes its motion to something else, even though it is itself the cause of motion in another thing, may cease to be in motion and therefore cease to live. Only what moves itself never ceases to be in motion, since it could not so cease without being false to its own nature; it is the source and prime origin of movement in all other things that move. Now a prime origin cannot come into being; all that comes into being must derive its existence from a prime origin, but the prime origin itself from nothing; for if a prime origin were derived from anything, it would no longer be a prime origin.[2]

Moreover, since it does not come into being, it must also be indestructible; for since all things must be derived from a prime origin, if the prime origin is destroyed, it will not come into being again out of anything, nor any other thing out of it. So we see that the prime origin of motion is what moves itself, and this can neither be destroyed nor come into being: otherwise the whole universe and the whole creation would collapse and come to a stop, and there would be nothing by which it could again be set in motion and come into existence. Now, since it has been proved that what moves itself is immortal, a man need feel no hesitation in identifying it with the essence and definition of soul. For all body which has its source of motion outside itself is soulless; but a body which moves itself from within is endowed with soul, since self-motion is of the very nature of soul. If then it is established that what moves itself is identical with soul, it inevitably follows that soul is uncreated and immortal.

246

1. The Greek is equally susceptible of the translations 'all soul' and 'every soul'. But 'the collective sense is that primarily demanded by the logic of the argument,' (Hackforth, *Plato's Phaedrus*, p. 64, n. 3).
2. Reading οὐκ ἂν ἔτι ἀρχὴ γίγνοιτο.

THE MYTH. THE ALLEGORY OF THE CHARIOTEER
AND HIS HORSES. THE PROCESSION OF THE
GODS AND THE VISION OF REALITY. THE
FALL, INCARNATION AND LIBERATION OF THE
SOUL. THE PRIVILEGE OF THE PHILOSOPHER.
RECOLLECTION AS A MEANS TO THE RECAPTURE
OF KNOWLEDGE OF THE FORMS.

*The argument just given for the immortality of soul is, like the final
argument of the* Phaedo, *a dialectical argument; Plato believes that
this is something which can be rigidly demonstrated. What soul is like,
however, and the nature of its existence can be described only in
symbols or what Plato terms a 'myth'. After the famous comparison
of the soul to a charioteer with two horses, a comparison which would
be hardly intelligible without knowledge of the psychological scheme of
Republic IV, where the three elements of reason, spirit and appetite
are distinguished, the myth proper begins with extreme abruptness with
the words 'Behold, first in the procession'. It must be remembered
that, though the myth is partly allegorical, there is much in it which is
purely poetical, particularly in the account of the procession of the
gods. This cannot be rationalized into an astronomical scheme, though
Hestia, the goddess of the hearth, symbolizes earth, and the statement
that she alone remains in the house of the gods is meant 'simply to
bring more vividly before the mind's eye the picture of the starry
heaven revolving round a fixed central body, the earth' (Hackforth,
op. cit., p. 73).*

SOCRATES: This must suffice concerning soul's immortality;
concerning its nature we must give the following account.
To describe it as it is would require a long exposition of
which only a god is capable; but it is within the power of
man to say in shorter compass what it resembles. Let us
adopt this method, and compare the soul to a winged
charioteer and his team acting together. Now all the horses
and charioteers of the gods are good and come of good
stock, but in other beings there is a mixture of good and bad.

First of all we must make it plain that the ruling power in us men drives a pair of horses, and next that one of these horses is fine and good and of noble stock, and the other the opposite in every way. So in our case the task of the charioteer is necessarily a difficult and unpleasant business.

Now we must try to tell how it is that we speak of both mortal and immortal living beings.[1] Soul taken as a whole is in charge of all that is inanimate, and traverses the entire universe, appearing at different times in different forms. When it is perfect and winged it moves on high and governs all creation, but the soul that has shed its wings falls until it encounters solid matter. There it settles and puts on an earthly body, which appears to be self-moving because of the power of soul that is in it, and this combination of soul and body is given the name of a living being and is termed mortal. There is not a single sound reason for positing the existence of such a being who is immortal, but because we have never seen or formed an adequate idea of a god, we picture him to ourselves as a being of the same kind as ourselves but immortal, a combination of soul and body indissolubly joined for ever. The existence of such beings and the use of such language about them we must leave to the will of God; let us pass on to consider the reason which causes a soul to shed and lose its wings; it is something like this.

The function of a wing is to take what is heavy and raise it up into the region above, where the gods dwell; of all things connected with the body, it has the greatest affinity with the divine, which is endowed with beauty, wisdom, goodness and every other excellence. These qualities are the prime source of nourishment and growth to the wings of the soul, but their opposites, such as ugliness and evil, cause the wings to waste and perish. Behold, first in the procession, driving his winged team, goes Zeus the mighty leader of the heavenly array, whose providence orders and

1. The question arises because soul has been shown to be immortal. By a 'living being' Plato means a being with a body informed by a soul.

watches over all things. There follows him a host of gods and spirits marshalled in eleven bands; for Hestia alone remains behind in the house of the gods, while the rest of the twelve ruler gods[1] lead on their companies, each in the station which is appointed for him. Now many glorious sights meet the eyes of the blessed gods on the journeys to and fro beneath the vault of heaven which they take in pursuit each of his allotted task, and they are followed by whoever is able and willing to follow them, since jealousy has no place in the company of the divine. But when they go to the celebration of their high feast day, they take the steep path leading to the summit of the arch which supports the outer heaven. The teams of the gods, which are well matched and tractable, go easily, but the rest with difficulty; for the horse with the vicious nature, if he has not been well broken in, drags his driver down by throwing all his weight in the direction of the earth; supreme then is the agony of the struggle which awaits the soul.

Now the souls that are termed immortal, when they reach the summit of the arch, go outside the vault and stand upon the back of the universe; standing there they are carried round by its revolution while they contemplate what lies outside the heavens. But of this region beyond the skies no mortal poet has sung or ever will sing in such strains as it deserves. Nevertheless the fact is this; for we must have the courage to speak the truth, especially when truth itself is our theme. The region of which I speak is the abode of the reality with which true knowledge is concerned, a reality without colour or shape, intangible but utterly real, apprehensible only by intellect which is the pilot of the soul.[2] So the mind of a god, sustained as it is by pure intelligence and knowledge, like that of every soul which is destined to

1. The twelve 'ruler gods' are presumably the twelve Olympians, to whom an altar existed at Athens. Some have interpreted them as deities controlling the twelve signs of the Zodiac. But what is then to be made of the position of Hestia?

2. cf. the description of the Form of Beauty in *Symposium* 210E.

assimilate its proper food, is satisfied at last with the vision of reality, and nourished and made happy by the contemplation of truth, until the circular revolution brings it back to its starting-point. And in the course of its journey it beholds absolute justice and discipline and knowledge, not the knowledge which is attached to things which come into being, nor the knowledge which varies with the objects which we now call real, but the absolute knowledge which corresponds to what is absolutely real in the fullest sense. And when in like manner it has beheld and taken its fill of the other objects which constitute absolute reality, it withdraws again within the vault of heaven and goes home. And when it comes home the charioteer sets his horses at their manger and puts ambrosia before them and with it a draught of nectar to drink.

Such is the life of the gods. But of the other souls that 248
which is likest to a god and best able to follow keeps the head of its charioteer above the surface as it makes the circuit, though the unruly behaviour of its horses impairs its vision of reality. A second class sometimes rises and sometimes sinks, and owing to the restiveness of its horses sees part, but not the whole. The rest, in spite of their unanimous striving to reach the upper world, fail to do so, and are carried round beneath the surface, trampling and jostling one another, each eager to outstrip its neighbour. Great is the confusion and struggle and sweat, and many souls are lamed and many have their wings all broken through the feebleness of their charioteers; finally, for all their toil, they depart without achieving initiation into the vision of reality, and feed henceforth upon mere opinion.[1]

The reason for their extreme eagerness to behold the plain of truth is that the meadow there produces fit pastur-

---

1. Opinion (*doxa*) is constantly opposed by Plato to knowledge (*episteme*), which is to be attained only by the pursuit of philosophy. But *doxa* has the further implication of 'appearance' contrasted with 'reality'; hence for Plato the sensible world can give rise only to *doxa*, and *episteme* is confined to knowledge of the real world of the Forms.

age for the best part of the soul, and that the wings by which the soul is borne aloft are nourished by it. And it is decreed by fate that any soul which has attained some vision of truth by following in the train of a god shall remain unscathed till the next great circuit, and if it can continue thus for ever shall be for ever free from hurt. But when a soul fails to follow and misses the vision, and as the result of some mishap sinks beneath its burden of forgetfulness and wrong-doing, so that it loses its wings and falls to earth, the law is this. In its first incarnation no soul is born in the likeness of a beast; the soul that has seen the most enters into a human infant who is destined to become a seeker after wisdom or beauty or a follower of the Muses and a lover; the next most perceptive is born as a law-abiding monarch or as a warrior and commander; the third as a man of affairs or the manager of a household or a financier; the fourth is to be a lover of physical activity or a trainer or physician; the fifth is given the life of a soothsayer or an official of the mysteries; the sixth will make a poet or a practitioner of some other imitative art; the seventh an artisan or a farmer; the eighth a popular teacher or a demagogue; the ninth a tyrant.[1]

In all this the lot which befalls a man between two incarnations corresponds to the goodness or badness of his previous life. The individual soul does not return whence it came for ten thousand years; so long does it take for a soul to grow its wings again, except it be the soul of one who has sought after wisdom without guile or whose love for a boy has been combined with such a search. These souls, if they choose the life of the philosopher three times successively, regain their wings in the third period of a thousand years, and in the three-thousandth year win their release. The rest at the end of their first life are brought to

249

1. The fall of the soul and its reincarnation are Pythagorean and Orphic concepts which deeply influenced Plato. Tyranny and the tyrant are the worst of all the political constitutions and corresponding types of personality in Books VIII and IX of the *Republic*. cf. also *Gorgias*, pp. 468ff.

judgement, and after judgement some go to expiate their
sins in places of punishment beneath the earth, while others
are borne aloft by justice to a certain region of the heavens
to enjoy the reward which their previous life in human form
has earned. But in the thousandth year both sorts alike
must draw lots and make choice of their second life, each
soul according to its own pleasure.[1] At this moment a
human soul may take upon itself the life of a beast, or a soul
which was originally human may change from beast back
to man. It is impossible for a soul that has never seen the
truth to enter into our human shape; it takes a man to
understand by the use of universals, and to collect out of the
multiplicity of sense-impressions a unity arrived at by a
process of reason.[2] Such a process is simply the recollection
of the things which our soul once perceived when it took its
journey with a god, looking down from above on the
things to which we now ascribe reality and gazing upwards
towards what is truly real. That is why it is right that the
soul of the philosopher alone should regain its wings; for
it is always dwelling in memory as best it may upon those
things which a god owes his divinity to dwelling upon. It is
only by the right use of such aids to recollection, which
form a continual initiation into the perfect mystic vision
that a man can become perfect in the true sense of the word.
Because he stands apart from the common objects of human
ambition and applies himself to the divine, he is reproached

1. The section of the myth which concerns judgement and punishment
or reward should be compared with the myth of Er at the end of the
Republic, with which it has much in common, in particular the combination of lot and choice in the determination of lives. The fact that this
combination, here mentioned without comment, is fully explained in the
myth of Er constitutes a powerful argument for dating the *Republic*
before the *Phaedrus*.

2. Knowledge of a Form, e.g. of beauty, is arrived at by consideration
of the various objects of experience which partake of it. For a full description of this process in the case of beauty cf. *Symposium* 210ff. The idea that
sensible objects constitute 'reminders' of the Forms which the soul knew
before its incarnation is first developed in the *Meno*.

by most men for being out of his wits; they do not realize that he is in fact possessed by a god.

This then is the fourth type of madness, which befalls when a man, reminded by the sight of beauty on earth of the true beauty, grows his wings and endeavours to fly upward, but in vain, exposing himself to the reproach of insanity because like a bird he fixes his gaze on the heights to the neglect of things below; and the conclusion to which our whole discourse points is that in itself and in its origin this is the best of all forms of divine possession, both for the subject himself and for his associate, and it is when he is touched with this madness that the man whose love is aroused by beauty in others is called a lover. As I have said, every human soul by its very nature has beheld true being – otherwise it would not have entered into the creature we call man – but it is not every soul that finds it easy to use its present experience as a means of recollecting the world of reality. Some had but a brief glimpse of the truth in their former existence; others have been so unfortunate as to be corrupted by evil associations since they fell to earth, with the result that they have forgotten the sacred vision they once saw. Few are left who retain a sufficient memory. These, however, when they see some likeness of the world above, are beside themselves and lose all control, but do not realize what is happening to them because of the dimness of their perceptions.

Now the earthly likenesses of justice and self-discipline and all the other forms which are precious to souls keep no lustre, and there are few who by the use of their feeble faculties and with great difficulty can recognize in the counterfeits the family likeness of the originals. But beauty was once ours to see in all its brightness, when in the company of the blessed we followed Zeus as others followed some other of the Olympians, to enjoy the beatific vision and to be initiated into that mystery which brings, we may say with reverence, supreme felicity. Whole were we who celebrated that festival, unspotted by all the evils which awaited us in time to come, and whole and unspotted and changeless and serene were the objects revealed to us in the light of that mystic vision. Pure was the light and pure were we from the pollution of the walking sepulchre which we call a body, to which we are bound like an oyster to its shell.

LOVE IS THE REGROWTH OF THE WINGS OF THE SOUL. THE DIFFERENT TYPES OF LOVER.

SOCRATES: So much by way of tribute to memory, whose revival of our yearning for the past has led us far afield. But beauty, as we were saying, shone bright in the world above, and here too it still gleams clearest, even as the sense by which we apprehend it is our clearest. For sight is the keenest of our physical senses, though it does not bring us knowledge. What overpowering love knowledge would inspire if it could bring as clear an image of itself before our sight, and the same may be said of the other forms which are fitted to arouse love. But as things are it is only beauty which has the privilege of being both the most clearly discerned and the most lovely. Now the man who is not fresh from his initiation or who has been corrupted does not quickly make the transition from beauty on earth to absolute beauty; so when he sees its namesake here he feels no reverence for it, but surrenders himself to sensuality and is eager like a four-footed beast to mate and to beget children, or in his addiction to wantonness feels no fear or shame in pursuing a pleasure which is unnatural. But the newly initiated, who has had a full sight of the celestial vision, when he beholds a god-like face or a physical form which truly reflects ideal beauty, first of all shivers and experiences something of the dread which the vision itself inspired; next he gazes upon it and worships it as if it were a god, and, if he were not afraid of being thought an utter mad-man, he would sacrifice to his beloved as to the image of a divinity. Then, as you would expect after a cold fit, his

251

57

condition changes and he falls into an unaccustomed sweat; he receives through his eyes the emanation of beauty, by which the soul's plumage is fostered, and grows hot, and this heat is accompanied by a softening of the passages from which the feathers grow, passages which have long been parched and closed up, so as to prevent any feathers from shooting. As the nourishing moisture falls upon it the stump of each feather under the whole surface of the soul swells and strives to grow from its root; for in its original state the soul was feathered all over. So now it is all in a state of ferment and throbbing; in fact the soul of a man who is beginning to grow his feathers has the same sensations of pricking and irritation and itching as children feel in their gums when they are just beginning to cut their teeth.

When in this condition the soul gazes upon the beauty of its beloved, and is fostered and warmed by the emanations which flood in upon it – which is why we speak of a 'flood' of longing – it wins relief from its pain and is glad; but when it is parched by separation the openings of the passages where the feathers shoot close up through drought and obstruct the development of the new growth. Imprisoned below the surface together with the flood of longing of which I have spoken, each embryo feather throbs like a pulse and presses against its proper outlet, so that the soul is driven mad by the pain of the pricks in every part, and yet feels gladness because it preserves the memory of the beauty of its darling. In this state of mingled pleasure and pain the sufferer is perplexed by the strangeness of his experience and struggles helplessly; in his frenzy he cannot sleep at night or remain still by day, but his longing drives him wherever he thinks that he may see the possessor of beauty. When he sees him and his soul is refreshed by the flood of emanations the closed passages are unstopped; he obtains a respite from his pains and pangs, and there is nothing to equal the sweetness of the pleasure which he enjoys for the moment. From this state he never willingly emerges; in his eyes no one can compare with his beloved; mother, brothers, friends, all are forgotten, and if his property is lost through his negligence he thinks nothing of it; the conventions of civilized behaviour, on whose observance he used to pride himself, he now scorns; he is ready to be a slave and to make his bed as near as he is allowed to the object of his passion; for besides the reverence which he feels for the possessor of beauty he has found in him the only physician for sickness of the most grievous kind. This sickness, let me inform the handsome lad whom I am supposed to be addressing, men call *eros*, but the gods have a name for it which in his youthful ignorance he will probably laugh at. There are two lines on love quoted by the admirers of Homer from the apocryphal works, of which the second is highly bizarre and not free from defects of metre. They go as follows:

Eros the god that flies is his name in the language of mortals:

But from the wings he must grow he is called by celestials Pteros.[1]

You may believe this or not as you like, but the cause and the effect of what happens to lovers are as I have described.

The burden imposed by the god who takes his name from wings is borne with greater dignity if the bearer be one who followed in the train of Zeus. But those who attached themselves to Ares and made the circuit with him, if they fall a prey to love and conceive themselves to be injured by the object of their passion, thirst for blood and are ready to sacrifice both their own lives and their favourite's.[2] Simil-

---

1. Pteros is an imaginary name derived from *pteron* (wing). Its initial consonants are responsible for the defect in metre, and the lines may be an adaptation from lines by some previous writer ascribed to Homer.

2. The object of this paragraph seems to be to allow for the existence of true lovers who yet are not philosophers. Plato has perhaps particularly in mind the pairs of lovers common in the Spartan army and of whom the Sacred Band of Thebes was composed. They are praised by Phaedrus in his speech in the *Symposium* (179C). Later in the *Phaedrus* (256C) Plato

arly with the other gods; every man during his first incarnation on earth, as long as he remains uncorrupted,
spends his time in worshipping and doing his best to
imitate the particular god whose devotee he was, and
conducts himself accordingly in his dealings with those he
loves and with the rest of the world. So in selecting his love
from among the possessors of beauty each man follows his
own bent, and, treating his beloved as if he were himself a
god, he fashions and adorns an image, metaphorically
speaking, and makes it the object of his honour and worship. Now those who were followers of Zeus desire a
Zeus-like disposition in the person they are to love; they
look for a temperament in which love of wisdom is combined with ability to lead, and when they find it they fall in
love and do everything in their power to encourage its
natural tendency. If they have not previously embarked on
this pursuit, they now apply themselves to the discovery of
truth from every available source of knowledge and from
their own personal researches; they find in themselves
traces by which they can detect the nature of the god to
whom they belong, and their task is facilitated by the
necessity which constrains them to keep their eyes fixed
upon him; by the aid of memory they lay hold on him and
are possessed by him, so that they take from him their
character and their way of life, in so far as it is possible for a
man to partake of divinity. Believing that their beloved is
the cause of this they cherish him all the more, and whatever
draughts of inspiration they draw from Zeus they pour out
like Bacchants[1] over the soul of their darling, and so make

253

allows some merit even to physical lovers in certain circumstances. But
in general his attitude to physical homosexuality is one of emphatic
condemnation. It has to be admitted that this passage, especially in what
it says of the followers of Ares, cannot be comfortably accommodated to
Plato's treatment of love in the rest of this speech and in Diotima's speech
in the *Symposium*.

1. The point of the comparison seems to be that the follower of Zeus
imparts his inspiration to his associate in the same way as the devotees of
Bacchus impart their frenzy to one another.

him as like as possible to the god they serve. Those who follow in the train of Hera look for a kingly disposition in the object of their choice, and when they find it act towards it in every respect like the followers of Zeus. And so with the followers of Apollo and of each of the other gods: every man desires to find in his favourite a nature comparable to his own particular divinity, and when he lights upon such a one he devotes himself to personal imitation of his god and at the same time attempts to persuade and train his beloved to the best of his power to walk in the ways of that god and to mould himself upon him. There is no room for jealousy or mean spite;[1] his whole effort is concentrated upon leading the object of his love into the closest possible conformity with himself and with the god he worships. This is the aspiration of the true lover, and this, if he succeeds in gaining his object in the way I describe, is the glorious and happy initiation which befalls the beloved when his affections are captured by a friend whom love has made mad. Now the manner of his capture is this.

THE CHARIOTEER ALLEGORY RESUMED. THE SUBJUGATION OF APPETITE, TYPIFIED BY THE BAD HORSE, AND THE AWAKENING OF LOVE FOR THE LOVER IN THE BELOVED. A CONCLUDING PRAYER TO THE GOD FOR LYSIAS AND PHAEDRUS.

SOCRATES: Let us abide by the distinction we drew at the beginning of our story, when we divided each soul into three elements, and compared two of them to horses and the third to their charioteer. One of the horses, we say, is good and one not; but we did not go fully into the excellence of the good or the badness of the vicious horse, and that is what we must now do. The horse that is harnessed on the senior side is upright and clean-limbed; he holds his

1. Jealousy has been attributed to the lover both by Lysias (232D) and by Socrates in his first speech (239A).

neck high and has a somewhat hooked nose; his colour is white, with black eyes; his thirst for honour is tempered by restraint and modesty; he is a friend to genuine renown and needs no whip, but is driven simply by the word of command. The other horse is crooked, lumbering, ill-made; stiff-necked, short-throated, snub-nosed; his coat is black and his eyes a bloodshot grey; wantonness and boastfulness are his companions, and he is hairy-eared and deaf, hardly controllable even with whip and goad. Now when the charioteer sees the vision of the loved one, so that a sensation of warmth spreads from him over the whole soul and he begins to feel an itching and the stings of desire, the obedient horse, constrained now as always by a sense of shame, holds himself back from springing upon the beloved; but the other, utterly heedless now of the driver's whip and goad, rushes forward prancing, and to the great discomfiture of his yoke-fellow and the charioteer drives them to approach the lad and make mention of the sweetness of physical love. At first the two indignantly resist the idea of being forced into such monstrous wrong-doing, but finally, when they can get no peace, they yield to the importunity of the bad horse and agree to do what he bids and advance. So they draw near, and the vision of the beloved dazzles their eyes. When the driver beholds it the sight awakens in him the memory of absolute beauty; he sees her again enthroned in her holy place attended by chastity. At the thought he falls upon his back in fear and awe, and in so doing inevitably tugs the reins so violently that he brings both horses down upon their haunches; the good horse gives way willingly and does not struggle, but the lustful horse resists with all his strength. When they have withdrawn a little distance the good horse in shame and dread makes the whole soul break into a sweat, but the other no sooner recovers from the pain of the bit and of his fall than he bursts into angry abuse, reproaching the driver and his fellow horse for their cowardice and lack of spirit in running away and breaking their word. After one more attempt to force his unwilling partners to advance he grudgingly assents to their entreaty that the attempt should be deferred to another time. When that time comes they pretend to forget, but he reminds them; forcing them forward, neighing and tugging, he compels them to approach the beloved once more with the same suggestion. And when they come near he takes the bit between his teeth and pulls shamelessly, with head down and tail stretched out. The driver, however, experiences even more intensely what he experienced before; he falls back like a racing charioteer at the barrier, and with a still more violent backward pull jerks the bit from between the teeth of the lustful horse, drenches his abusive tongue and jaws with blood, and forcing his legs and haunches against the ground reduces him to torment. Finally, after several repetitions of this treatment, the wicked horse abandons his lustful ways; meekly now he executes the wishes of his driver, and when he catches sight of the loved one is ready to die of fear. So at last it comes about that the soul of the lover waits upon his beloved in reverence and awe.

Thus the beloved finds himself being treated like a god 255 and receiving all manner of service from a lover whose love is true love and no pretence, and his own nature disposes him to feel kindly towards his admirer. He may repulse him at first because in the past he has imbibed from school-fellows and others the mistaken idea that it is disgraceful to have dealings with a lover, but as time goes on his increasing maturity and the decree of destiny bring him to admit his lover to his society; after all it is not ordained that bad men should be friends with one another, nor yet that good men should not. When he has made him welcome and begun to enjoy his conversation and society, the constant kindness that he meets with in close companionship with his lover strikes the beloved with amazement; he realizes clearly that all his other friends and relations together cannot offer him anything to compare with the affection that he receives from this friend whom a god has inspired. When their intimacy is established and the loved one has grown used to being near his friend and touching him in the gymnasium and elsewhere, the current of the stream which Zeus when he was in love with Ganymede called the 'stream of longing' sets in full flood towards the lover. Part of it enters into him, but when his heart is full the rest brims over, and as a wind or an echo rebounds from a smooth and solid surface and is carried back to its point of origin, so the stream of beauty returns once more to its source in the beauty of the beloved. It enters in at his eyes, the natural channel of communication with the soul, and reaching and arousing the soul it moistens the passages from which the feathers shoot and stimulates the growth of wings, and in its turn the soul of the beloved is filled with love.

So now the beloved is in love, but with what he cannot tell. He does not know and cannot explain what has happened to him; he is like a man who has caught an eye-infection from another and cannot account for it; he does not realize that he is seeing himself in his lover as in a glass. In his lover's presence he feels a relief from pain like his; when he is away he longs for him even as he himself is longed for. He is experiencing a counter-love which is the reflection of the love he inspires, but he speaks of it and thinks of it as friendship, not as love. Like his lover, though less strongly, he feels a desire to see, to touch, to kiss him, and to share his bed. And naturally it is not long before these desires are fulfilled in action. When they are in bed together, the lover's unruly horse has a word to say to his driver, and claims to be allowed a little enjoyment in return for all that he has suffered. But his counterpart in the beloved has nothing to say; but swelling with a desire of whose nature he is ignorant he embraces and kisses his lover as a demonstration of affection to so kind a friend, and when they are in each other's arms he is in a mood to refuse no favour that the lover may ask; yet his yoke-fellow in his turn joins with the charioteer in opposing to this impulse the moderating influence of modesty and reason. So, if the higher elements in their minds prevail, and guide them into a way of life which is strictly devoted to the pursuit of wisdom, they will pass their time on earth in happiness and harmony; by subduing the part of the soul that contained the seeds of vice and setting free that in which virtue had its birth they will become masters of themselves and their souls will be at peace. Finally, when this life is ended, their wings will carry them aloft; they will have won the first of the three bouts in the real Olympian Games, the greatest blessing that either human virtue or divine madness can confer on man.

But if they practise a less exalted way of life and devote themselves to the pursuit of honour rather than of wisdom,[1] it may come about that in their cups or at some other unguarded moment their two unruly beasts will catch them unaware, and joining forces constrain them to snatch at what the world regards as the height of felicity and to consummate their desire. Once they have enjoyed this pleasure they will enjoy it again thereafter, but sparingly, because what they do does not carry with it the consent of their whole mind. Though their friendship is upon a lower plane, such a pair too will remain friends, not only while their passion lasts but after it has abated; they will regard themselves as having exchanged mutual pledges so sacred that they can never without great guilt break them and become enemies. In the end they emerge from the body without wings, it is true, but having made a strong effort to achieve them; this is no mean prize, and it comes to them from the madness of love. Those who have already begun their heavenward journey the law does not compel to go down into the darkness beneath the earth: they pass their time journeying happily together in the brightness of day, and together, when the time comes, they receive their wings, because of their love.

Such, my son, are the divine blessings which will accrue to you from the friendship of a lover. But intimacy with one

1. cf. above p. 59, n. 2.

who is not in love, mingled as it is with worldly calculation and dispensing worldly advantages with a grudging hand, will breed in your soul the ignoble qualities which the multitude extols as virtues, and condemn you to wander for nine thousand years around and beneath the earth devoid of wisdom.

257

This speech, dear God of Love, I offer to thee in reparation as the best and finest palinode that my powers can devise. If its language in particular is perforce the language of poetry, the responsibility lies at Phaedrus' door. Grant me forgiveness for my former words and let these that I have now uttered find favour in thy sight. Deal kindly and graciously with me, and do not in anger take away or impair the skill in the science of love[1] which thou hast given me; rather let me increase in honour in the sight of those that have beauty. If in the beginning Phaedrus and I uttered aught that offended thy ears, lay it to the account of Lysias the true begetter of that speech and make him cease from such words; turn his heart to the love of wisdom, even as the heart of Polemarchus his brother is turned,[2] so that this his loving disciple[3] may no longer be in two minds, as he is now, but may employ his life in philosophic discussion directed towards love in singleness of heart.

INTRODUCTION TO THE DISCUSSION OF RHETORIC.
THE MYTH OF THE CICADAS.

The transition to the second part of the dialogue is effected by making Phaedrus express a doubt whether Lysias will be willing to attempt another speech to match that of Socrates. He has been reproached with being a speech-writer. Socrates replies that all men in public life practise what is in effect speech-writing; there can therefore be

1. Socrates makes a similar claim in the *Symposium* 177D, 212B.
2. Polemarchus is responsible for capturing Socrates at the opening of the *Republic* and the dialogue is set in his house at Piraeus.
3. Phaedrus.

nothing inherently disgraceful in it; what is important is to disting-uish between good writing and speaking and the reverse. The effect of this is to extend the discussion to include every kind of persuasive use of words, not simply what was generally regarded as rhetoric. Lysias' critic meant to abuse him as a writer of speeches for the law courts (logographos), and Socrates' bland assumption that logographos has a much wider meaning than that given to it in current usage is characteristic.

The consideration of rhetoric in this extended sense is postponed while Socrates relates a short and charming myth, designed perhaps to emphasize that divine aid is as important for the discussion of rhetoric as for that of love.

PHAEDRUS: I say Amen to that prayer, Socrates; so may it be if so it is best for us. All this time I have been lost in wonder at the immense superiority of this speech over that which preceded it; indeed, I am afraid that Lysias may appear feeble in comparison, supposing that he is prepared to match against it another speech of his own. But in fact, my dear Socrates, one of our politicians was recently making this very thing the subject of a diatribe against Lysias; the sum of all his reproaches was that Lysias is a writer of speeches. So it may be that regard for his reputa-tion will keep him from writing any more.

SOCRATES: A preposterous notion, my dear young man. You are far astray in your judgement of your friend if you suppose him a man to be frightened by mere words. But perhaps you think that his critic really meant what he said to be a reproach?

PHAEDRUS: He certainly gave me that impression. And you yourself, Socrates, are perfectly well aware, I'm sure, that those who occupy the positions of greatest power and dignity in our states are ashamed to write speeches or to leave written compositions behind them, because they are afraid that posterity may give them the name of sophists.

SOCRATES: It's a case of Pleasant Bend, Phaedrus. You've forgotten that it is the *long* bend in the Nile which gives rise to that euphemism,[1] and you've forgotten too that the politicians with the highest opinion of themselves are the most passionately anxious to write speeches and leave compositions behind them; why, whenever they write anything, they are so keen to win approval that they preface it with a clause containing the names of those who approve whatever that particular speech may contain.

PHAEDRUS: What do you mean? I don't follow you.

258 SOCRATES: Aren't you aware that any document composed by a politician is headed by the names of those who approve it?

PHAEDRUS: Explain yourself.

SOCRATES: 'Resolved', he begins, 'by the Council' or 'by the Assembly' or by both, and then goes on 'Moved by so-and-so,' a splendidly pompous bit of self-advertisement on the part of the author. After that comes the body of his proposal, in which he displays his own wisdom to his supporters, sometimes in a composition of considerable length. Can you describe a document of this kind as anything but a speech committed to writing?

PHAEDRUS: No.

SOCRATES: Well, if he carries the day, the author leaves the stage triumphant, but if his motion is rejected and he loses his position as a recognized writer of speeches of this kind, he and his friends are plunged in gloom.

PHAEDRUS: They are indeed.

SOCRATES: Obviously their attitude to this occupation is one of admiration, not of contempt.

PHAEDRUS: Unquestionably.

SOCRATES: Again, when an orator or a king reaches a position of power like Lycurgus[2] or Solon or Darius, and acquires immortality in his country as a writer of speeches, does he

1. There were various explanations of this proverb. Here it is clearly meant by Plato as an illustration of the truth that men sometimes say the opposite of what they mean. Lysias' critic is such a person.

2. Lycurgus is the traditional founder of the Spartan constitution; Solon the Athenian law-giver; and Darius the famous King of Persia defeated at the Battle of Marathon.

not in his own life-time think himself the equal of the gods, and does not posterity agree in this estimate of him when it contemplates his productions?

PHAEDRUS: Certainly.

SOCRATES: Do you think then that any man of affairs, whoever he may be and however much an enemy of Lysias, seriously holds it against him that he is an author?

PHAEDRUS: Not if what you say is true, for in that case he would be criticizing his own darling pursuit.

SOCRATES: Then it must be clear to everybody that there is nothing inherently disgraceful in speech-writing.

PHAEDRUS: Agreed.

SOCRATES: The disgrace comes, I take it, when one speaks and writes disgracefully and badly instead of well.

PHAEDRUS: Obviously.

SOCRATES: How then are we to distinguish between good and bad writing? Shall we have to consult Lysias on the subject or any one else who has written or is going to write? The nature of the writing does not signify; it may be on either public or private matters, either in verse or prose.

PHAEDRUS: Shall we have to consult, you ask. What would be the point of existing at all if it were not for pleasures such as these? Certainly life is not worth living for pleasures whose enjoyment entirely depends on a previous sensation of pain, like almost all physical pleasures; that is why the latter are rightly called the pleasures of slaves.

SOCRATES: Well, we seem to have time at our disposal. What is more, I cannot help fancying that the cicadas overhead, singing and chattering to one another as their habit is in stifling heat, are watching us too. If they were to see us doing what most people do in the middle of the day, nodding under their soothing spell from sheer mental indolence instead of conversing, they would be entitled to laugh at us; they would take us for a pair of slaves that had invaded their haunt and were taking their mid-day nap near the spring, like sheep. But if they see us in conversation and realize that we are as deaf to their spells as if we

259

were sailing past the Sirens, it may be that in admiration they will grant us the boon which heaven allows them to confer on mortal men.

PHAEDRUS: What boon is that? I don't think I have heard of it.

SOCRATES: It is most unfitting that a lover of the Muses should be ignorant of such a matter. The story is that once, before the birth of the Muses, cicadas were human beings. When the Muses were born and song came into the world, some of the men of that age were so ravished by its sweetness that in their devotion to singing they took no thought to eat and drink, and actually died before they knew what was happening to them. From them sprang thereafter the race of cicadas, to whom the Muses granted the privilege that they should need no food, but should sing from the moment of birth till death without eating and drinking, and after that go to the Muses and tell how each of them is honoured on earth and by whom. So the cicadas make report to Terpsichore of those who have honoured her in the dance, and thus win her favour for them; to Erato of those who have occupied themselves in matters erotic, and similarly to the other Muses, according to the nature of the activity over which each Muse presides. But to Calliope the eldest of the Muses and her next sister Urania they make report of those who spend their lives in philosophy and honour the pursuit which owes its inspiration to these goddesses; among the Muses it is these that concern themselves with the heavens and the whole story of existence, divine and human, and their theme is the finest of them all. So you see that there are many reasons why we should proceed with our discussion instead of indulging in a mid-day sleep.

PHAEDRUS: Of course we must proceed with it.

SOCRATES: Then we must examine the question we propounded just now, what constitutes excellence and its opposite in speaking and writing.

PHAEDRUS: That is obvious.

THE NECESSITY OF KNOWLEDGE FOR A
TRUE ART OF RHETORIC

Socrates sets out to convince Phaedrus that, contrary to the common opinion which Phaedrus shares, any genuine art of persuasion requires knowledge of the subject of which the speaker is treating. Even a speaker who wishes to mislead will only be successful in doing so in so far as he is not misled himself. The speech of Lysias, apart from its technical defects, fails because Lysias himself has no clear grasp of the meaning of the ambiguous word 'love'.

This treatment of rhetoric, expanded to include any form of argument, forensic, deliberative, or logical, which aims at producing conviction, should be compared with the treatment of the same subject in the Gorgias. *That Plato means the reader to have this in mind is shown by the description of rhetoric at* 260E *as a 'knack which has nothing to do with art', a phrase which he has already employed in* Gorgias 463B *as a generic name for the practice of 'pandering' of which he there treats rhetoric as a sub-division. But, whereas in the* Gorgias *rhetoric is totally condemned as a bastard art, the* Phaedrus *is concerned to establish the possibility of a genuine art of persuasion which is based on knowledge.*

SOCRATES: Well, if a speech is to be classed as excellent, does not that presuppose knowledge of the truth about the subject of the speech in the mind of the speaker?

PHAEDRUS: But I have been told, my dear Socrates, that what a budding orator needs to know is not what is really right, but what is likely to seem right in the eyes of the mass of people who are going to pass judgement: not what is really good or fine but what will seem so; and that it is this rather than truth that produces conviction.

SOCRATES: 'Not to be lightly regarded',[1] Phaedrus, is any word from the lips of the wise. On the contrary, we must see whether they may not be right, and in particular we must not dismiss what you have just said.

PHAEDRUS: Quite so.

1. Homer, *Iliad* 2.361.

260

SOCRATES: Let us look at it like this.

PHAEDRUS: How?

SOCRATES: Suppose I am trying to persuade you to buy a horse for service on a campaign. Neither of us knows exactly what a horse is, but I happen to know this much about you – Phaedrus believes a horse to be the longest-eared of the domestic animals.

PHAEDRUS: A ludicrous idea, Socrates.

SOCRATES: Wait a moment. Suppose that in a serious effort to persuade you I make use of a piece that I have composed in praise of the donkey. I call the donkey a horse, and tell you that the beast is highly serviceable both at home and in the field; you can use it to fight on, and to carry your baggage besides, and for many other purposes.

PHAEDRUS: That would be the height of absurdity.

SOCRATES: Isn't it better to be an absurd friend than a clever enemy?

PHAEDRUS: Of course.

SOCRATES: Well, when a speaker who does not know the difference between good and evil tries to convince a people as ignorant as himself, not by ascribing to a poor beast like a donkey the virtues of a horse, but by representing evil as in fact good, and so by a careful study of popular notions succeeds in persuading them to do evil instead of good, what kind of harvest do you think his rhetoric will reap from the seed he has sown?

PHAEDRUS: No very satisfactory harvest, I should say.

SOCRATES: But can it be, my friend, that we have treated the art of speech-making more roughly than we should? Perhaps she might reply: 'What nonsense is this, my good sirs? I do not insist on ignorance of truth as an essential qualification for the would-be speaker; for what my advice is worth I suggest that he should acquire that knowledge before embarking on me.[1] I do emphatically assert, however,

1. cf. *Gorgias* 460A, where Gorgias, though he has disclaimed responsibility for the use made by his pupils of his rhetorical teaching, admits that if a pupil came to him ignorant of the nature of right and wrong he would feel bound to teach him.

that without my assistance the man who knows the truth will make no progress in the art of persuasion.'

PHAEDRUS: If she says that, will she not be right?

SOCRATES: Yes, if the arguments that she still has to encounter support her claim to be an art. I think I hear some of them approaching and testifying that she is lying, and that she is not an art at all but a knack which has nothing to do with art. There is not nor ever shall be, as the Spartan said, a genuine art of speaking which is divorced from grasp of the truth.[1]

PHAEDRUS: We need these arguments, Socrates. Bring them on and ask them what they mean. 261

SOCRATES: Come forward, noble creatures, and persuade Phaedrus, who begets such lovely children,[2] that unless he becomes an adequate philosopher he will never be an adequate speaker either on any subject. And let Phaedrus answer.

PHAEDRUS: Ask your questions.

SOCRATES: Well, to give a general definition, is not the art of rhetoric a method of influencing men's minds by means of words, whether the words are spoken in a court of law or before some other public body or in private conversation? And is not the same art involved whatever the importance of the subject under discussion, so that it is no more creditable to use it correctly on a serious matter than on a trifle? Is that what you have been told of its nature?

PHAEDRUS: Oh no, not quite that. Lectures and writings on rhetoric as an art generally confine themselves to forensic oratory, though sometimes the former include political oratory as well. I have never heard the term used in a wider sense than that.

SOCRATES: Can it be that you have heard only of the treatises on the art of speaking composed by Nestor and Odysseus

1. The apophthegm is probably Plato's own, but the Spartans were renowned both for apophthegms (hence our use of 'laconic') and for dislike of rhetoric.

2. An allusion to Phaedrus as the originator of speeches.

PLATO

in their moments of leisure at Troy, and never of that of
Palamedes?

PHAEDRUS: I have never heard even of that of Nestor, unless
you are casting Gorgias for the part of Nestor, and Thrasymachus or Theodorus for that of Odysseus.¹

SOCRATES: Perhaps I am. But never mind them for the
moment. Tell me, what is it that the opposing parties in a
court of law engage in? Can we call it anything but a verbal
contest?

PHAEDRUS: No, that is exactly what it is.

SOCRATES: About what is just and unjust?

PHAEDRUS: Yes.

SOCRATES: Then the man who follows the rules of the art
will make the same jury think the same action just one
moment and unjust the next, as he pleases?

PHAEDRUS: Of course.

SOCRATES: And in political speeches he will make his
audience approve a course of action at one time and reject
the same course at another?

PHAEDRUS: He will.

SOCRATES: But what about our Palamedes from Elea? Isn't
it well known that he employs an art of speaking which
makes his hearers think that the same objects are both like
and unlike, both one and many, both at rest and in motion?²

PHAEDRUS: True.

SOCRATES: Then the art of controversy is not confined to

---

1. Nestor is the eloquent 'elder statesman' of the Iliad, and Gorgias
resembled him in both eloquence and longevity. Odysseus is famous for
subtlety and resource, but the exact point of the comparison with Thrasymachus or Theodorus is obscure. Palamedes, whose name signifies
'inventor' and who was famous for his discoveries, is generally identified
with Zeno the Eleatic, whose method of argument was to draw contra-
dictory conclusions from the same premise. Socrates' purpose is to emphasize that this kind of skill in argument is also to be included under the
generic title of rhetoric.

For Thrasymachus and Theodorus cf. p. 82. n. 2.

2. Zeno's method is illustrated in Plato's *Parmenides*. cf. Cornford, F. M.,
Plato and Parmenides, pp. 57ff.

law or politics; every kind of discussion, it appears, is covered by one and the same art, if it is an art, and by means of it a man can make anything appear like anything else within the limits of possible comparison, and expose an opponent when he attempts to perform the same feat without being detected.

PHAEDRUS: What is all this leading to?

SOCRATES: We shall see, I think, if we ask the following question. Is a great or a slight difference between two things the more likely to be misleading?

PHAEDRUS: A slight difference.

262

SOCRATES: So if you proceed by small degrees from one thing to its opposite you are more likely to escape detection than if you take big steps.

PHAEDRUS: Of course.

SOCRATES: Then a man who sets out to mislead without being misled himself must have an exact knowledge of the likenesses and unlikenesses between things.

PHAEDRUS: That is essential.

SOCRATES: If he does not know the true nature of any given thing, how can he discover in other things a likeness to what he does not know, and decide whether the resemblance is small or great?

PHAEDRUS: He cannot.

SOCRATES: Now, when people's opinions are inconsistent with fact and they are misled, plainly it is certain resemblances that are responsible for mistakes creeping into their minds.

PHAEDRUS: Yes, that is how it happens.

SOCRATES: Is it possible then for a man to be skilled in leading the minds of his hearers by small gradations of difference in any given instance from truth to its opposite, or to escape being misled himself, unless he is acquainted with the true nature of the thing in question?

PHAEDRUS: Quite impossible.

SOCRATES: It seems then, my friend, that the art of speaking displayed by a man who has gone hunting after opinions instead of learning the truth will be a pretty ridiculous sort of art, in fact no art at all.

PHAEDRUS: It looks like it.

SOCRATES: Would you like us then to look at some examples of what we call genuine art and its opposite in the speech of Lysias which you are carrying and in the speeches which we delivered?

PHAEDRUS: There is nothing I should like better. At present we are arguing in the abstract for lack of suitable illustrations.

SOCRATES: Well, by a lucky accident the two speeches[1] provide an example of how a speaker who knows the truth can make fun of his hearers and lead them astray. My own belief, Phaedrus, is that the local divinities are responsible for this; or it may be the interpreters of the Muses, the sweet singers overhead, that have been kind enough to inspire us, since for my part I lay no claim to any proficiency in the art of speaking.

PHAEDRUS: Put it down to them if you like; only please explain your meaning.

SOCRATES: Read me again the opening of Lysias' speech.

PHAEDRUS: 'You know my situation, and you have heard how I think that it will be to our advantage for this to happen. I beg you not to reject my suit because I am not in love with you. Lovers repent –'

SOCRATES: That will do. Now where does Lysias go wrong and show absence of art? That is what we have to demonstrate, isn't it?

PHAEDRUS: Yes.

SOCRATES: Well, is it not perfectly obvious that there are some words about which we are in agreement, and others about which we differ?

PHAEDRUS: I think I see your meaning, but amplify it, please.

1. It appears that Socrates is here speaking of Lysias' speech and his own *first* speech, or else that he is treating both his own speeches as one.

SOCRATES: When someone uses the words 'iron' or 'silver' we all have the same idea in our minds, haven't we?

PHAEDRUS: Certainly.

SOCRATES: But suppose the words used are 'just' or 'good'. Don't we then go each his own way, and find ourselves in disagreement with ourselves as well as with each other?

PHAEDRUS: Undoubtedly.

SOCRATES: So in some cases we are in agreement and in others not.

PHAEDRUS: Yes.

SOCRATES: In which case are we more liable to be misled, and in which is the art of speaking more effective?

PHAEDRUS: When the meaning of the word is uncertain, obviously.

SOCRATES: Then the man who embarks on the search for an art of speaking must first of all make a methodical classification, and find a distinguishing mark for each of the two kinds of words, those which in popular usage are bound to be ambiguous and those which are not.

PHAEDRUS: The man who grasps that will have made a very fine discovery, Socrates.

SOCRATES: Next, when he has to deal with a given subject, it must be perfectly clear to him, without any possibility of mistake, to which class the subject of his speech belongs.

PHAEDRUS: Of course.

SOCRATES: What of love then? Is it to be classified as ambiguous or unambiguous?

PHAEDRUS: Ambiguous, obviously. Otherwise, how would it have been possible for you to describe it as you did just now as a curse to lover and loved alike, and then to turn round and assert that it is the greatest of blessings?

SOCRATES: An excellent point. But tell me – I've been so carried out of myself that I've quite forgotten – did I define love at the beginning of my speech?

PHAEDRUS: You did indeed, in the most emphatic manner conceivable.

SOCRATES: Dear me, by your account the nymphs of Achelous and Pan the son of Hermes[1] are much greater experts in the art of speaking than Lysias the son of Cephalus. Or am I wrong, and did Lysias at the start of his encomium compel us to conceive of love as a definite thing on the meaning of which he had decided, and did he bring everything else in the whole course of his speech into conformity with that decision? Would you care to read his opening once more?

PHAEDRUS: As you please, but what you are looking for isn't there.

SOCRATES: Read it all the same, so that I can hear his own words.

PHAEDRUS: 'You know my situation, and you have heard how I think that it will be to our advantage for this to happen. I beg you not to reject my suit because I am not in love with you. Lovers repent the kindnesses they have shown when their passion abates.'

SOCRATES: You see how far Lysias is from doing what we are looking for. He is like a man swimming on his back, in reverse; his speech begins where it should have ended, and his opening words are what the lover should say to his darling when his speech is finished. Or am I mistaken, my dear Phaedrus?

PHAEDRUS: I grant you that what he is talking of is what one would expect to find in a peroration, Socrates.

SOCRATES: Then again, don't the various parts of his speech give the impression of being thrown together at random? Do you see any intrinsic reason why the second topic, rather than any of the others, should be placed second? I am an ignoramus, of course, but it seemed to me that the writer showed a fine carelessness by saying whatever occurred to him. Can you point out any compelling rhetorical reason why he should have put his arguments together in the order he has?

PHAEDRUS: You do me too much honour if you suppose that I am capable of divining his motives so exactly.

1. The divinities by whom Socrates professes to be inspired.

SOCRATES: But I think you would agree that any speech ought to have its own organic shape, like a living being; it must not be without either head or feet; it must have a middle and extremities so composed as to fit one another and the work as a whole.

PHAEDRUS: Of course.

SOCRATES: Well, now look at your friend's speech and see whether it conforms to this criticism. You will find that it is no better than the epitaph said to have been inscribed on the tomb of Midas the Phrygian.

PHAEDRUS: What epitaph is that and what is the matter with it?

SOCRATES: It goes like this:

> 'A girl of bronze on Midas' tomb I stand,
> As long as water flows and trees grow tall,
> Remaining here on his lamented tomb,
> I'll tell to all who pass "Here Midas lies"'[1]

You notice, I am sure, that it is of no consequence what order these lines are spoken in.

PHAEDRUS: You are making fun of our speech, Socrates.

THE SPEECHES OF SOCRATES ILLUSTRATE A NEW PHILOSOPHICAL METHOD

The knowledge on which a true rhetoric must be based is of course knowledge of the eternal realities, the Forms and soul; there is for Plato no other knowledge worthy of the name. For the moment, however, Socrates concentrates on a single principle which he claims to have exemplified in his two speeches: the method of defining a topic for discussion by 'collection' and 'division' or as we should say, by genus *and* species. *This method, to which he gives the name of dialectic, is announced by Socrates with the enthusiasm proper to a new discovery, and it plays a prominent part in dialogues later than the* Phaedrus, *notably the* Sophist, Politicus, *and* Philebus. *It has been suggested[2] that one of the main purposes of the dialogue is to announce this*

1. This epigram was attributed by some in antiquity to Cleobulus of Lindus, who occurs in some lists of the Seven Sages.
2. Hackforth, op cit., p. 134.

method, which must be distinguished from the dialectic sketched in the Republic. *That was concerned with the ascent of the philosopher from sensible particulars to Forms and ultimately to the Form of Good, and the subsequent deduction of all truth from this single principle. Its culminating point is a mystical experience, which can be described only by analogies. The* Phaedrus *is here concerned with something much more practical, the use of definitions by* genus *and* species *as an aid to clarity and precision of thought.*

The distinction between 'right-hand' and 'left-hand' love which Socrates is enabled to make by the application of this method explains the transition from the condemnation of love in his first speech to the eulogy in the second. But it is to be noted that in neither speech is the method employed with anything like the exactness specified in the present passage; it is only in the second that Socrates begins with the generic concept of madness, and even there there is no scheme of successive division; he proceeds from genus *to* infima species *in a single step.*

SOCRATES: Well, I don't want to vex you, so we will let it pass, although it seems to me to contain a number of features which an observer would profit by not attempting to imitate. Let us turn to the other speeches; they contained something, I think, worth the attention of the student of rhetoric.

PHAEDRUS: What do you mean?

SOCRATES: They were, you remember, opposites; one maintained that a lover's desires should be gratified, and the other a non-lover's.

PHAEDRUS: And in both cases you argued like a man.

SOCRATES: I thought you were going to say like a madman, which would be no more than the truth. And that brings me to the very point I wished to make. We said that love was a kind of madness, didn't we?

PHAEDRUS: Yes.

SOCRATES: And that there are two types of madness, one arising from human disease, the other when heaven sets us free from established convention.

PHAEDRUS: Agreed.

SOCRATES: And we distinguished four kinds of divine madness and ascribed them to four divinities,[1] the inspiration of the prophet to Apollo, that of the mystic to Dionysus, that of the poet to the Muses, and the fourth kind to Aphrodite and Love; and of the four we declared the last, the madness of the lover, to be the best. And in trying to tell what the emotion of love is like it may be that we hit upon some truth, though in some respects perhaps we went astray. Anyhow, the mixture resulted in a not entirely unconvincing speech, a mythical hymn which celebrates in suitably devotional language the praises of Love, who is your master and mine, Phaedrus, and the protector of the young and fair.

PHAEDRUS: I certainly took great pleasure in hearing it.

SOCRATES: Let us then concentrate our attention on this single point, the way in which the transition from blame to praise was effected.

PHAEDRUS: What do you mean to deduce from that?

SOCRATES: My view is that, though the rest of the speech was really no more than a *jeu d'esprit*, yet in its random utterances two methods of reasoning can be discerned, and that it would be no bad thing if one could get a clear scientific idea of their function.

PHAEDRUS: What are these methods?

SOCRATES: The first method is to take a synoptic view of many scattered particulars and collect them under a single generic term, so as to form a definition in each case and make clear the exact nature of the subject one proposes to expound. So in our recent speech on love we began by defining what love is. That definition may have been good or bad, but at least it enabled the argument to proceed with clearness and consistency.

1. This is not a wholly accurate recapitulation of the classification made at 244, in which Apollo was alluded to only by implication and Dionysus not mentioned at all.

PHAEDRUS: What is the other method you have in mind, Socrates?

SOCRATES: The ability to divide a genus into species again, observing the natural articulation, not mangling any of the parts, like an unskilful butcher. Take my two speeches just now. Both took irrationality as a generic notion. But just as in a single physical body there are pairs of organs with the same name but distinguished as left and right respectively, so in our two speeches: both postulated madness as a single generic form existing in us, but the first separated the left-hand part, as it were, and broke it down into further parts and did not give up till it detected among them what may be called a left-hand kind of love, which it very properly reprobated; whereas the second directed our attention to the types of madness on the right-hand side, and, finding there a kind of love which has the same name as the other but is divine, held it up before our eyes and eulogized it as the source of the greatest blessings that can fall to our lot.

PHAEDRUS: Perfectly true.

SOCRATES: Well, Phaedrus, I am a great lover of these methods of division and collection as instruments which enable me to speak and to think, and when I believe that I have found in anyone else the ability to discuss unity and plurality as they exist in the nature of things, I follow in his footsteps 'like the footsteps of god'.[1] Hitherto I have given those who possess this ability the title of dialecticians, though heaven knows if I am right to do so. It is for you now to tell me what one ought to call them if one takes yourself and Lysias for one's masters. Can it be that what I have been describing is precisely that art of rhetoric to which Thrasymachus[2] and the rest owe their ability not only to speak themselves but to make a good speaker of any-

1. An adaptation of a Homeric phrase.
2. Aristotle mentions Thrasymachus of Chalcedon as the second of a trio of early technical writers on rhetoric, the others being Tisias and Theodorus. He is best known from the first book of the *Republic*, where he is made to maintain, like Callicles in the *Gorgias*, that Might is Right.

one who is prepared to pay them tribute as if they were kings?

PHAEDRUS: They may behave like kings, but they are quite ignorant of the kind of knowledge you are asking about. You are quite right, I am sure, to give the name of dialectic to the method you have described, but I believe that the nature of rhetoric is still eluding us.

SOCRATES: How can that be? Is there anything worth having that can be systematically acquired if it is divorced from dialectic? If so, you and I should certainly not despise it. But what is rhetoric, what is left of it? That is the question that must be answered.

PHAEDRUS: There is a great deal left, Socrates, the whole contents, in fact, of the technical treatises on the subject.

A REVIEW OF THE DEVICES AND TECHNICAL TERMS OF CONTEMPORARY RHETORIC

This review, to a modern reader perhaps the least attractive part of the dialogue, leads to the conclusion that what pass as the rules of rhetoric are in fact no more than preliminaries to the practice of the true art.

SOCRATES: Thank you for reminding me. The first point, I suppose, is that a speech must begin with an 'introduction'. That is the sort of thing you mean, isn't it, the technical refinements of composition?

PHAEDRUS: Yes.

SOCRATES: Next must come a 'statement of the facts' supported by the evidence of witnesses; after that 'indirect evidence'; fourthly 'arguments from probability'; not to mention the 'proof' and 'supplementary proof' distinguished by that expert in rhetorical subtlety from Byzantium.

PHAEDRUS: Are you referring to the worthy Theodorus?

SOCRATES: Of course I am. And besides these one must 267 include a 'refutation' and a 'subsidiary refutation', whether one is acting for the prosecution or the defence. And are we to leave out of account the admirable Evenus of Paros,[1] the inventor of 'insinuation' and 'indirect compliments'? Some say that he also composed metrical examples of 'indirect blame', to serve as mnemonics – there was no end to the cleverness of the man. Then there are Tisias[2] and Gorgias. Shall we leave buried in oblivion men who saw that probability is to be rated higher than truth, and who could make trivial matters appear great and great matters trivial simply by the forcefulness of their speech, besides discovering how to clothe new ideas in fine old language and to refurbish old thoughts by novel treatment, and to speak on any subject either compendiously or at infinite length? Once, however, when Prodicus[3] heard me talking of this last accomplishment, he burst out laughing, and declared that he alone had found the secret of artistic oratory, which is that speeches should be neither long nor short but of suitable compass.

PHAEDRUS: Well done, Prodicus – what a brilliant discovery!

SOCRATES: And what of Hippias? The stranger from Elis would agree, I think, with Prodicus.

PHAEDRUS: Undoubtedly.

SOCRATES: Then there is Polus.[4] What are we to say of his *Muses' Treasury of Speech*, with its 'Style Repetitive', its 'Style Sententious', and its 'Style Metaphorical', not to speak of the terms Licymnius presented him with as a contribution to his ornate style?

1. A poet as well as a sophist, mentioned in *Phaedo* 60D and *Apology* 20B as being alive at the time.

2. Tisias (early fifth century) was one of the founders of the Sicilian school of rhetoric and the teacher of Gorgias of Leontini. Gorgias was an extreme sceptic, and his use of probability as a criterion may be associated with his denial of the existence of objective truth.

3. Prodicus and Hippias of Elis (and, of course, Protagoras) are sophists characterized at some length in the *Protagoras* pp. 337ff.

4. A pupil of Gorgias, whom he replaces as Socrates' interlocutor in the *Gorgias*. Little is known of Licymnius, though his fondness for superfluous technicalities is mentioned with disapproval by Aristotle *Rhetoric* 3.13.

PHAEDRUS: But was there not something similar by Protagoras, Socrates?

SOCRATES: Yes, my lad, you mean his *Correct Diction*, and many other admirable works. But in the art of composing pathetic speeches bearing upon old age and poverty the master of them all in my opinion is the mighty man of Chalcedon.[1] He was expert also in rousing a crowd to fury, and then soothing its fury again by the spell of his words, to use his own expression; and in casting aspersions and removing them on any grounds or none he was unrivalled. To pass on, however. There seems to be general agreement about the ending of a speech; some call it recapitulation, while others give it different names.

PHAEDRUS: You mean refreshing the memory of the audience by giving at the end a brief summary of the various points in the speech?

SOCRATES: Exactly. Now is there anything else that you would like to add about the art of rhetoric?

PHAEDRUS: Only a few things hardly worth mentioning.

SOCRATES: Then never mind them. Let us rather hold what we have got up to the light, and examine what effect these technicalities produce and on what occasions.

PHAEDRUS: A very powerful effect, Socrates, at any rate in popular assemblies.

SOCRATES: No doubt. But look close, my good friend, and see whether the texture of the stuff seems as threadbare to you as it does to me.

PHAEDRUS: I should like you to demonstrate it.

SOCRATES: Very well. Now, if someone came to your friend Eryximachus or his father Acumenus[2] and said that by the application of certain substances to the body of a patient he could induce at will heat or cold, or, if he thought fit, vomiting or purging, and so on, and by virtue of this knowledge claimed to be a doctor or to be able to make a

1. Thrasymachus. cf. p. 82, n. 2.
2. cf. p. 21, n. 1.

PLATO

doctor of anyone to whom he imparted it, what do you
think his hearers would say?

PHAEDRUS: Obviously they would ask whether he also knew
what patients should be subjected to each of these treat-
ments, and when, and to what extent.

SOCRATES: Suppose he were to answer: 'Of course not. I
expect my pupil to be able to find out what you ask for
himself.'

PHAEDRUS: Then no doubt they would say: 'This man is
mad. He has read something in a book or lit upon certain
prescriptions by chance, and believes himself to be a doctor
when he knows nothing of the art of medicine.'

SOCRATES: Or suppose a man were to approach Sophocles
and Euripides and say that he knew how to compose
lengthy speeches about trifles and very concise ones about
matters of importance, and that he could turn out at will
passages of deep pathos or at the other extreme tirades full
of fury and menace, or produce any other effect to order,
and claimed that by imparting these skills he could in fact
deliver the recipe for a tragedy?

PHAEDRUS: As in the other instance, Socrates, his hearers
would doubtless laugh at a man who did not realize that
what makes a tragedy is the combination of these elements
in such a way as to harmonize with each other and with the
whole.

SOCRATES: But instead of indulging in vulgar abuse they
would, I am sure, be more likely to behave like a musician
when he encounters someone who, because he knows how
to strike the highest and lowest possible notes, believes that
he is a master of harmony. The musician will not say
roughly: 'My poor man, you're daft.' On the contrary,
being a musician he will use gentler language and say: 'It is
quite true, my good sir, that anyone who aspires to master
harmony must possess the knowledge you have acquired,
but a man in your position may for all that be quite ignorant
of harmony. What you have is not knowledge of harmony
but only an indispensable preliminary to such knowledge.'

86

PHAEDRUS: Absolutely right.

SOCRATES: So Sophocles would tell the man who was show-   269
ing off to him and Euripides that his ability was merely a
necessary preliminary to the tragic art, not the art itself, and
Acumenus would make a similar answer about medicine.

PHAEDRUS: Of course they would.

SOCRATES: Well then. Suppose that honey-tongued Adras-
tus[1] or even Pericles were to hear talk of these fine devices of
concise expression and metaphorical expression and the like,
which we said must be gone through and held up to the
light to be examined. Do you think they would imitate the
vulgar behaviour of people like you and me, and content
themselves with hurling a rough and uncultivated phrase at
those who have taught and written about these devices as
the whole art of rhetoric? Would they not rather, out of
their superior wisdom, find fault with us and say: 'Instead
of losing your temper, Phaedrus and Socrates, you should
make allowances for those who, because they do not
understand dialectical method, have proved unable to
define the nature of rhetoric, and have believed in consequence that they have discovered the art itself, when all that
they have got hold of is the knowledge which is a necessary
preliminary to it. They think that by imparting this knowledge they have perfectly discharged the task of a teacher of
rhetoric, and that the use of each of these devices so as to
produce conviction and the composition of a consistent
whole is a simple matter which their pupils must work out
for themselves when they come to make speeches.

PHAEDRUS: I believe you are right, Socrates. It looks as if the
art which such people teach and write about as the art of
rhetoric is no more than you say. But in that case how and
where is one to acquire the genuine art of the convincing
speaker?

1. A mythical king of Argos. The epithet comes from the poet Tyrtaeus,
and perhaps refers to his power of soothing the fury of Theseus. cf. the
Supplices of Euripides. It is possible, but by no means certain, that he
stands here for a contemporary rhetorician.

RHETORIC AND PHILOSOPHY

True rhetoric requires not only talent and practice, but also the training and method of the philosopher. Pericles, the most finished speaker in the world, owed this to his association with the philosopher Anaxagoras. In particular the true rhetorician must have a clear view of the nature of soul in general and of the various types of individual soul, and be able to adapt his arguments accordingly so as to produce conviction. Only then will he be a practitioner of the genuine art of rhetoric. There is no short cut to this achievement; the true method is certainly laborious, but its object is not merely to gratify one's fellow human beings but to carry into effect the will of the gods.

The association of Pericles with Anaxagoras is well known. It is not, however, obvious how Anaxagoras, a physical philosopher, for whom Mind is simply a cosmological principle, can have helped Pericles to a knowledge of human nature. Probably all that is meant is that Pericles acquired from Anaxagoras a philosophical outlook. Anaxagoras, like other pre-Socratics, looked for a fundamental substance underlying the manifold phenomena of the sensible world, and Plato's idea may be that Pericles was encouraged by this to base his rhetoric on a view of the essential nature of soul (as Hippocrates, Phaedrus suggests, based the art of medicine on a view of the essential nature of body).

The high praise given to Pericles as a speaker is in strong contrast with the bitterness with which he is condemned as a statesman in the Gorgias (515ff). It is true that he is here being considered as a speaker, not as a statesman, but it seems likely that Plato has modified the violence of his earlier view, formed when the condemnation of Socrates was still a recent memory.

SOCRATES: If you mean the power to become a finished performer, Phaedrus, it seems likely – indeed, inevitable – that what is true of everything else holds good here also. If you have a natural gift for speaking you will become a famous speaker, provided that you improve your gift by knowledge and practice, but if any of these conditions is unfulfilled you will to that extent fall short of your goal. In so far as it is a matter of art the method which appeals to me is not the method which is pursued by Lysias and Thrasymachus.

PHAEDRUS: What is it then?

SOCRATES: I fancy, my friend, that it was not surprising that Pericles became the most finished speaker who has ever lived.

PHAEDRUS: Why do you say that?

SOCRATES: All the great arts need to be supplemented by philosophical chatter and daring speculation about the nature of things: from this source appear to come the sublimity of thought and all-round completeness which characterize them. Now Pericles added these qualities to his own natural gifts; he fell in with Anaxagoras, who was a thinker of this type, and by steeping himself in speculation arrived at a knowledge of the nature of reason and unreason,[1] the favourite subject, no doubt, of Anaxagoras' discourse, from which Pericles drew and applied to the art of speaking whatever was relevant to it.

PHAEDRUS: How do you mean?

SOCRATES: The same is presumably true of the art of rhetoric as of the art of medicine.

PHAEDRUS: In what way?

SOCRATES: In both cases a nature needs to be analysed, in one the nature of the human body and in the other the nature of the soul. Without this any attempt to implant health and strength in the body by the use of drugs or diet, or the kind of conviction and excellence you desire in the soul by means of speeches and rules of behaviour, will be a matter of mere empirical knack and not of science.

PHAEDRUS: You may well be right, Socrates.

SOCRATES: Now do you think it possible to form an adequate conception of the nature of an individual soul without considering the nature of soul in general?

PHAEDRUS: If we are to believe the Asclepiad doctor Hippo-

1. Reading ἀνοίας.

PLATO

crates[1] this method is equally essential in dealing with an
individual body.

SOCRATES: Hippocrates is quite right, my friend. But Hippocrates' authority is not enough; we must see whether sound
reason is on his side.

PHAEDRUS: Of course.

SOCRATES: What then have Hippocrates and Truth to say on
this subject? Surely that if we are to form a clear notion of
the nature of anything at all, we must first determine
whether the subject on which we wish to acquire scientific
knowledge ourselves and the ability to impart that knowledge to others is simple or complex. Next, if it is simple we
must examine its natural function, both active and passive;
what does it act upon and what acts upon it? If it is complex
we must determine the number of its parts, and in the case
of each of these go through the same process as applies to
the simple whole; how and on what does it produce an
effect, and how and by what is an effect produced upon
it?

PHAEDRUS: It may be as you say, Socrates.

SOCRATES: Any other procedure would be like the groping
of a blind man. We must not expose the scientific investiga-
tor of any subject to a comparison with the blind – or with
the deaf, for that matter. Now, plainly, if one is to teach the
art of speaking on scientific lines, one must demonstrate
precisely the essential nature of the object to which the art is
to be applied, and that object, I presume, is soul.

PHAEDRUS: Of course.

271   SOCRATES: Then it is towards soul that all the rhetorician's
energy will be directed. It is there he aims to produce
conviction, is it not?

PHAEDRUS: Yes.

SOCRATES: So it is clear that Thrasymachus and any other

1. All physicians are Asclepiads, because the god Asclepius was the
founder of the art of medicine. It is not possible to identify the source of
Phaedrus' statement in the numerous extant works attributed to Hippocrates.

serious and scientific teacher of the art of speaking will regard it as his first duty to make us see as precisely as possible whether soul is naturally a homogeneous unity or complex, like body; that is what we mean by demonstrating its nature.

PHAEDRUS: Certainly.

SOCRATES: In the next place he will describe how and upon what it naturally acts, and how and by what it is acted upon, and to what effect.

PHAEDRUS: No doubt.

SOCRATES: Thirdly, he will classify the various types of speech and of soul, and the ways in which souls can be affected, and arrange them in corresponding pairs, giving reasons for his choice and showing why a particular sort of speech inevitably produces conviction in a particular sort of soul, and fails to do so in another.

PHAEDRUS: That would be the best way, it seems.

SOCRATES: Not merely the best but the only way, my dear Phaedrus; no other method of demonstration in speech or writing can be called scientific, whatever the subject it deals with. The existing writers of rhetorical manuals, whose lectures you have heard, are rogues: they are perfectly well aware of the truth about soul but choose to keep it from us. So we must not admit their claim to be scientific until they speak and write in the way I describe.

PHAEDRUS: What way do you mean?

SOCRATES: To give the actual words would be too much of a business, but I don't mind telling you how one ought to write if one wants to be as scientific as possible.

PHAEDRUS: Please do.

SOCRATES: The function of speech is to influence the soul. It follows that the would-be speaker must know how many types of soul there are. The number is finite, and they account for the variety of individual characters. When these have been determined one must enumerate the various types of speech, a finite number also. For such and such a reason a certain type of person can be easily persuaded to adopt a certain course of action by a certain type of speech, whereas for an equally valid reason a different type cannot. When the student has an adequate theoretical knowledge of these types, the next requisite is that his powers of observation should be keen enough to follow them up when he comes across them in actual life; otherwise he will be no better off for all the instruction received in the lecture room. When he is not only qualified to say what type of man is influenced by what type of speech, but is able also to single out a particular individual and make clear to himself that there he has actually before him a specific example of a type of character which he has heard described, and that this is what he must say and this is how he must say it if he wants to influence his hearer in this particular way – when, I say, he has grasped all this, and knows besides when to speak and when to refrain, and can distinguish when to employ and when to eschew the various rhetorical devices of conciseness and pathos and exaggeration and so on that he has learnt, then and not till then can he be said to have perfectly mastered his art. If his teaching or writing falls short in any of these respects we are entitled to reject his claim to be a properly qualified speaker. 'So', our writer on this subject may say to us, 'here is my account of the art of speaking, Phaedrus and Socrates; are you satisfied with it, or do you want something different?'

PHAEDRUS: One cannot ask for anything different, Socrates. Nevertheless what is set before us is no small task.

SOCRATES: You are quite right. Before we undertake it we should make a thorough review of all we have said on the subject, in case there should be a quicker and easier way to our goal. A long, rough, roundabout route would be a waste of time if there is a short and smooth one. So if what you have heard from Lysias or anyone else can help us at all here, do your best to recollect it.

PHAEDRUS: It's not for want of trying, but I have nothing to offer at the moment.

SOCRATES: Would you like me then to give you an account of

the matter which I heard from some who concern themselves with it?

PHAEDRUS: Of course.

SOCRATES: We are told, you know, Phaedrus, that it is
legitimate to play the devil's advocate.

PHAEDRUS: Then please do so.

SOCRATES: Well, to their way of thinking there is no need to
be so portentous or long-winded, or to make such uphill
work of the matter. The fact is, as we said at the beginning
of our discussion, that the aspiring speaker needs no
knowledge of the truth about what is right or good, or
about men whose nature or breeding has made them so. In
courts of justice no attention whatever is paid to the truth
about such topics; all that matters is plausibility. Plausibility is simply another name for probability, and probability
is the thing to concentrate on if you would be a scientific
speaker. There are even some occasions when both prosecution and defence should positively suppress the facts in
favour of probability, if the facts are improbable. Never
mind the truth – pursue probability through thick and thin
in every kind of speech; the whole secret of the art of
speaking lies in consistent adherence to this principle.   273

PHAEDRUS: This is what those who claim to be professional
teachers of rhetoric actually say, Socrates. We touched
briefly on this point at an earlier stage, I remember, and
those who make this their concern attach crucial importance
to it.

SOCRATES: Well, take Tisias; you've no doubt studied his
book carefully. Let us ask Tisias then whether he means by
probable anything more than what the public finds acceptable.

PHAEDRUS: What more could he mean?

SOCRATES: So it was as a result of this profound discovery
about his art that Tisias wrote that if a brave pygmy is
prosecuted for assaulting a cowardly giant and robbing him
of his clothes neither of them should reveal the truth. The
coward must declare that he was attacked by more than one

man, whereas his opponent must maintain that no one else was present and fall back on the well-known line: 'How could a little chap like me have set upon a colossus like him?' The other of course will not admit his own poor spirit, but will produce some further lie which may provide his adversary with a chance of tripping him. And in other cases too these are the sort of 'scientific' rules that are enunciated. Isn't it so, Phaedrus?

PHAEDRUS: Unquestionably.

SOCRATES: Dear me, what a strangely recondite art we owe to the invention of Tisias or whoever it was and whatever he was pleased to take his name from.[1] But, my dear Phaedrus, shall we or shall we not say to him –

PHAEDRUS: What?

SOCRATES: 'Tisias, for some time before you ever came on the scene we were saying that what you call probability establishes itself in the minds of the populace because of its likeness to truth; and we concluded that in every case such likenesses are best discovered by the man who knows the truth. So if you have anything further to say about the art of speaking we shall be glad to hear it; otherwise we shall accept the conclusion we have already reached that a man who does not distinguish the various natures among his audience, and who cannot analyse things into their species and classify individuals under a single form will never attain such mastery of the art of speaking as is open to man. This, however, is a goal that cannot be reached without great pains, which the wise man will undergo not with the object of addressing and dealing with human beings but in order to be able to the best of his power to say and do what is acceptable in the sight of heaven. Those who are wiser than we, Tisias, tell us that the object of a man of sense will not be the gratification of fellow-slaves, except incidentally, but of masters who are supremely good. It is no wonder then that the road is long and winding; the end to which it

274

1. Plato hints that the real inventor of rhetoric may have been not Tisias but Corax, whose name means *crow*, a bird of prey.

leads is a great end, different from the end which you propose to yourself; yet that, too, as our discussion shows, will best be reached, if a man has a mind to it, as a result of the other.'

PHAEDRUS: A magnificent theory, Socrates, I agree, if one could put it into practice.

SOCRATES: It is noble to aim at a noble goal, whatever the outcome.

PHAEDRUS: It is indeed.

SOCRATES: So much then for the genuine art of speaking and its opposite.

PHAEDRUS: Agreed.

THE INFERIORITY OF THE WRITTEN TO THE SPOKEN WORD

The dialogue ends with a discussion of the comparative merits of speech and writing as vehicles for the communication of truth. Like the discussion of rhetoric as a whole it is introduced by a short myth, but it is intimately connected with what has preceded it. cf. Introduction, pp.—10f.

SOCRATES: There remains the question of the propriety and impropriety of writing, and the conditions which determine them. We have still to discuss that, haven't we?

PHAEDRUS: Yes.

SOCRATES: Do you know the theory and practice which will best please God, as far as words are concerned?

PHAEDRUS: No, I do not. Do you?

SOCRATES: Well, I can give you a tradition handed down from men of old, but they alone know the truth. If we could find that out for ourselves, should we have any further use for human fancies?

PHAEDRUS: An absurd question. But tell me your tradition.

SOCRATES: They say that there dwelt at Naucratis[1] in Egypt

1. A Greek trading station from early times, mentioned by Herodotus as the only foreign port in Egypt.

one of the old gods of that country, to whom the bird they call Ibis was sacred, and the name of the god himself was Theuth.[1] Among his inventions were number and calculation and geometry and astronomy, not to speak of various kinds of draughts and dice, and, above all, writing. The king of the whole country at that time was Thamus, who lived in the great city of Upper Egypt which the Greeks call Egyptian Thebes; the name they give to Thamus is Ammon. To him came Theuth and exhibited his inventions, claiming that they ought to be make known to the Egyptians in general. Thamus inquired into the use of each of them, and as Theuth went through them expressed approval or disapproval, according as he judged Theuth's claims to be well or ill founded. It would take too long to go through all that Thamus is reported to have said for and against each of Theuth's inventions. But when it came to writing, Theuth declared: 'Here is an accomplishment, my lord the king, which will improve both the wisdom and the memory of the Egyptians. I have discovered a sure receipt for memory and wisdom.' 'Theuth, my paragon of inventors,' replied the king, 'the discoverer of an art is not the best judge of the good or harm which will accrue to those who practise it. So it is in this case; you, who are the father of writing, have out of fondness for your offspring attributed to it quite the opposite of its real function. Those who acquire it will cease to exercise their memory and become forgetful; they will rely on writing to bring things to their remembrance by external signs instead of on their own internal resources. What you have discovered is a receipt for recollection, not for memory. And as for wisdom, your pupils will have the reputation for it without the reality: they will receive a quantity of information without proper instruction, and in consequence be thought very knowledgeable when they are for the most part quite ignorant. And

275

1. Theuth is the Egyptian god Thoth, the 'scribe of the gods', to whom was attributed the invention of writing. He was a god of the second rank, whereas Thamus or Ammon was equated by the Greeks with Zeus.

because they are filled with the conceit of wisdom instead of real wisdom they will be a burden to society.'

PHAEDRUS: How easy you find it, Socrates, to compose a story from Egypt or any other country.

SOCRATES: Well, Phaedrus, the priests in the sanctuary of Zeus at Dodona[1] declared that the earliest oracles came from an oak tree, and the men of their time, who lacked your modern sophistication, were simple-minded enough to be quite satisfied with messages from an oak or a rock if only they were true. But truth is not enough for you; you think it matters who the speaker is and where he comes from.

PHAEDRUS: I accept the rebuke. What your Theban says about writing is quite sound, I'm sure.

SOCRATES: Then it shows great folly – as well as ignorance of the pronouncement of Ammon – to suppose that one can transmit or acquire clear and certain knowledge of an art through the medium of writing, or that written words can do more than remind the reader of what he already knows on any given subject.

PHAEDRUS: Quite right.

SOCRATES: The fact is, Phaedrus, that writing involves a similar disadvantage to painting. The productions of painting look like living beings, but if you ask them a question they maintain a solemn silence. The same holds true of written words; you might suppose that they understand what they are saying, but if you ask them what they mean by anything they simply return the same answer over and over again. Besides, once a thing is committed to writing it circulates equally among those who understand the subject and those who have no business with it; a writing cannot distinguish between suitable and unsuitable readers.[2] And if it is ill-treated or unfairly abused it always needs its parent to come to its rescue; it is quite incapable of defending or helping itself.

1. See p. 47, n. 1.
2. cf. Letter VII 341E.

PHAEDRUS: All that you say is absolutely just.

276 SOCRATES: Now can we distinguish another kind of communication which is the legitimate brother of written speech, and see how it comes into being and how much better and more effective it is?

PHAEDRUS: What kind do you mean and how does it come about?

SOCRATES: I mean the kind that is written on the soul of the hearer together with understanding; that knows how to defend itself, and can distinguish between those it should address and those in whose presence it should be silent.

PHAEDRUS: You mean the living and animate speech of a man with knowledge, of which written speech might fairly be called a kind of shadow.

SOCRATES: Exactly. Now tell me this. Would a sensible farmer take seed which he valued and wished to produce a crop, and sow it in sober earnest in gardens of Adonis at midsummer,[1] and take pleasure in seeing it reach its full perfection in eight days? Isn't this something that he might do in a holiday mood by way of diversion, if he did it at all? But where he is serious he will follow the true principles of agriculture and sow his seed in soil that suits it, and be well satisfied if what he has sown comes to maturity eight months later.

PHAEDRUS: You do well to distinguish, Socrates, between the farmer's serious business and what he might do in a different spirit.

SOCRATES: And are we to say that the man with real knowledge of right and beauty and good will treat what we may by analogy call his seed less intelligently than the farmer?

PHAEDRUS: Of course not.

SOCRATES: Then when he is in earnest he will not take a pen and write in water or sow his seed in the black fluid called

1. The festival of Adonis, who died untimely, was celebrated by forcing plants in shallow vessels, like our window-boxes, so that they produced blooms without being properly rooted.

ink, to produce discourses which cannot defend themselves
viva voce or give any adequate account of the truth.

PHAEDRUS: Presumably not.

SOCRATES: No, indeed. It will simply be by way of pastime
that he will use the medium of writing to sow what may be
styled gardens of literature, laying up for himself as well as
for those who follow the same track aids to recollection
against the time when the forgetfulness of old age may
overtake him, and it will give him pleasure to see the
growth of their tender shoots. And when other men resort to
other diversions, and indulge themselves with drinking-
parties and kindred pleasures, he on the contrary will
amuse himself, I think, with the sort of pastime that I am
describing.

PHAEDRUS: And a very fine pastime too, Socrates – as fine
as the other is worthless. I mean the ability to amuse oneself
with the composition of discourses about justice and the
other subjects you mention.

SOCRATES: Quite so, my dear Phaedrus. But finer still is the
serious treatment of these subjects which you find when a
man employs the art of dialectic, and, fastening upon a
suitable soul, plants and sows in it truths accompanied by
knowledge. Such truths can defend themselves as well as
the man who planted them; they are not sterile, but contain   277
a seed from which fresh truths spring up in other minds; in
this way they secure immortality for it, and confer upon the
man who possesses it the highest happiness which it is
possible for a human being to enjoy.

PHAEDRUS: The process you speak of is even more excellent.

SOCRATES: Then since that is agreed, Phaedrus, we can now
consider our original problem.

RECAPITULATION AND CONCLUSION

PHAEDRUS: What problem do you mean?

SOCRATES: The problem which has led us to the present
point in the search for its solution. We set out, if you

remember, to examine the reproach incurred by Lysias by reason of his speech-writing, and to determine what constitutes science and lack of science in speech-writing as a whole. The second point we have, I think, satisfactorily cleared up.

PHAEDRUS: So it appeared. But remind me once more how it was done.

SOCRATES: Our whole previous discussion has proved that speeches, whether their aim is to instruct or to persuade, cannot be scientifically constructed, in so far as their nature allows of scientific treatment at all, unless the following conditions are fulfilled. In the first place a man must know the truth about any subject that he deals with, either in speech or writing; he must be able to define it generically, and having defined it to divide it into its various specific kinds until he reaches the limit of divisibility. Next, he must analyse on the same principles the nature of soul, and discover what type of speech is suitable for each type of soul. Finally, he must arrange and organize his speech accordingly, addressing a simple speech to a simple soul, but to those which are more complex something of greater complexity which embraces the whole range of tones.

PHAEDRUS: There can be no doubt that that was the conclusion we reached.

SOCRATES: Then to return to the original point, whether the composition and delivery of speeches is honourable or dishonourable, and in what circumstances it may fairly be reckoned a reproach or the reverse. Has not our previous discussion plainly shown –

PHAEDRUS: What has it shown?

SOCRATES: That Lysias or any other writer, past or future, who claims that clear and permanently valid truth is to be found in a written speech, lays himself open to reproach, whether that reproach is actually levelled at him or not. It makes no difference whether the speech is to be delivered in a private capacity or in support of a constitutional proposal, when it becomes in effect a political treatise. To be unable to distinguish between dream and waking reality about right and wrong, good and evil, is a condition which cannot escape censure, even though the populace as a whole may be loud in its praise.

PHAEDRUS: Certainly it cannot.

SOCRATES: To believe, on the other hand, that a written composition on any subject must be to a large extent the creation of fancy; that nothing worth serious attention has ever been written in prose or verse – or spoken for that matter, if by speaking one means the kind of recitation that aims merely at creating belief, without any attempt at instruction by question and answer; that even the best of such compositions can do no more than help the memory of those who already know; whereas lucidity and finality and serious importance are to be found only in words spoken by way of instruction or, to use a truer phrase, written on the soul of the hearer to enable him to learn about the right, the beautiful and the good; finally, to realize that such spoken truths are to be reckoned a man's legitimate sons, primarily if they originate within himself, but to a secondary degree if what we may call their children and kindred come to birth, as they should, in the minds of others – to believe this, I say, and to let all else go is to be the sort of man, Phaedrus, that you and I might well pray that we may both become. 278

PHAEDRUS: What you say expresses exactly my own wish and prayer.

SOCRATES: Then I think we may be content with the literary discussion with which we have been amusing ourselves. Go and tell Lysias that we two went down to the stream and shrine of the Nymphs and there received the following message which we are charged to deliver to Lysias and other speech-writers, to Homer and other poets, whether they compose for accompaniment or not, and finally to Solon and anyone who has written treatises in the form of political utterances, which he calls laws. If any of them had knowledge of the truth when he wrote, and can defend what he has written by submitting to an interrogation on the subject, and make it evident as soon as he speaks how comparatively inferior are his writings, such a one should take his title not from what he has written but from what has been the object of his serious pursuit.

PHAEDRUS: What is the title you have in mind for him?

SOCRATES: To call him wise, Phaedrus, would, I think, be excessive; God alone deserves to be so described. But to call him a lover of wisdom or something of the sort would be more appropriate and at the same time more modest.

PHAEDRUS: There would be nothing amiss in that.

SOCRATES: Then the man whose most precious production is what he has composed or written, and who has devoted his time to twisting words this way and that, pasting them together and pulling them apart, may fairly be called a poet or a speech-writer or a maker of laws.

PHAEDRUS: Of course.

SOCRATES: That then is the message you must take to your friend.

PHAEDRUS: But what about you? You have a friend too, and it would be just as wrong to neglect him.

SOCRATES: Whom do you mean?

PHAEDRUS: The fair Isocrates. What message will you take to him, Socrates, and how shall we describe him?

SOCRATES: Isocrates is still young, Phaedrus. But I don't mind telling you the future I foresee for him.

279

PHAEDRUS: Please do.

SOCRATES: He seems to me to have natural gifts superior to anything displayed in the speeches of Lysias, and the elements in his character make a nobler combination. So I should not be at all surprised if, as he grows older, he makes all his predecessors in the kind of composition in which he is now engaged look like children, or if he becomes dissatisfied with his present pursuits and is driven on by some divine inspiration to greater things. Nature, my dear Phaedrus, has not left the man devoid of a certain love of wisdom. That is the message that I am taking from the divinities here to Isocrates, who is my favourite, and you must take the other to Lysias, who is yours.

PHAEDRUS: Very well. Let us be going then, since the heat has abated.

SOCRATES: Surely we should first make a prayer to the powers of this place.

PHAEDRUS: Of course.

SOCRATES: 'Dear Pan and ye other gods who inhabit here, grant that I may become fair within, and that my external circumstances may be such as to further my inward health. May I esteem the wise man rich, and allow me no more wealth than a man of moderation can bear and manage.' Is there anything else that we should ask for, Phaedrus? To me my prayer seems sufficient.

PHAEDRUS: Offer it for me too, Socrates; friends should share everything.

SOCRATES: Let us be going.

TWO PLATONIC LETTERS

*

Plato's written works include, in addition to the dialogues, a collection of thirteen letters. They have formed part of the Platonic canon since the first century A.D. and possibly since the third century B.C., and one in particular, the Seventh, which is as long as all the rest together, is a document of crucial importance for our knowledge of Plato's life. It opens with an account of his early development and of his reasons for abstaining from public affairs, and it records in detail the motives which led in later life to his famous and unsuccessful excursion into the practical politics of Sicily and his relations with Dionysius II of Syracuse. It may almost be said that without the Seventh Letter Plato's personal history would be unknown.

The authenticity of the letters cannot be regarded as established beyond question. Forged letters ascribed to famous names abounded in later antiquity, and for this reason alone all collections of ancient letters are open to some suspicion. Moreover, one at least of the Platonic collection is undoubtedly spurious. The most important of them, however, including the Seventh and Eighth, were accepted from early times as genuine: Cicero refers to the Seventh as 'that celebrated letter'[1] and Plutarch makes use of it explicitly in his life of Dion. In modern times the Third, Seventh, and Eighth Letters have been accepted as genuine by most Platonic scholars; there is nothing in their style and diction incompatible with Plato's later dialogues, and the arguments which have been brought against them are subjective and far from conclusive.[2] Nevertheless it has to be

1. *Tusculan Disputations* 5.100.
2. The most recent attack on the letters in general and the Seventh in particular is by Edelstein, L., *Plato's Seventh Letter*, Leyden, 1966. For a summary of the whole controversy cf. Raven, J. E., *Plato's Thought in the Making*, 1965, pp. 19–26.

recognized that there is an element of uncertainty in the matter; all that can be said is that the Seventh Letter in particular, if it is a forgery, is a forgery on a scale and of an elaboration otherwise unknown among forged letters, and if, as seems certain, it cannot date from a period far removed from Plato's own time there is no need to condemn the information which it contains as entirely unhistorical. The burden of proof rests on those who would reject it; further than this it may never be possible to go.

*

Plato's first visit to Sicily took place about 388 B.C., when he was forty years old. Dionysius I was in power at Syracuse, where he had established a military monarchy which at its greatest extent included most of the Greek cities of southern Italy and formed one of the most powerful autocracies in the Greek world. Supported by foreign mercenaries Dionysius kept at bay the Carthaginians who occupied the western tip of the island, but his rule was far from beneficial to the Sicilian Greeks in general; he had devastated and depopulated many of their cities in the interests of despotism, and though the forms of democracy were still observed at Syracuse he was in fact a dictator of the most absolute type, a tyrant in both ancient and modern senses of the word. His régime was of a type which Plato denounces unsparingly in the *Republic* and elsewhere, and the motive for Plato's first visit to his court is obscure; in the course of it, however, he formed a close friendship with Dion, a young man of about twenty, whose sister was one of Dionysius' two wives. Plato saw in Dion unusual gifts of character and intellect, and Dion was strongly attracted to Plato's philosophical views.

Twenty years later, in 367, Dionysius I died, and was succeeded by his son, Dionysius II, a man of some native ability who had been kept in obscurity and ignorance by his father, but in whom Dion saw a possibility of developing, with Plato's help, a philosophic ruler. He persuaded Dionysius to invite Plato to Syracuse, and Plato with some misgivings accepted the invitation. He was cordially received and established friendly relations with Dionysius, but the visit was unsuccessful. Three months after his arrival a quarrel between Dionysius and Dion ended in the exile of the latter, and, though Plato remained some time longer, he made no progress in influencing Dionysius in the face of determined opposition by the supporters of despotism. He left, however, with an understanding that both he and Dion should return at a later date, when Dionysius had made peace with the Carthaginians.

In 361 Dionysius invited Plato to return, though without honouring his undertaking to recall Dion, and much against his better judgement Plato agreed, partly, we are told, from a feeling that he must neglect no chance, however remote, of converting Dionysius, and partly in the hope of doing something to improve the situation of Dion. The events of this visit are described at length in the Seventh Letter.

It ended in total disappointment, and when Plato finally returned to Greece in 360 Dion decided to assert his rights by force. He landed in Sicily in 357 with a small mercenary army, was received with joy by the citizens of Syracuse, and succeeded without resistance in making himself master of the city, except for the impregnable island fortress of Ortygia, where Dionysius maintained himself. From this point disasters multiplied. Dion, who, whatever his intellectual gifts and his ability as a commander, seems to have been lacking in the qualities needed to conciliate popular support and to manage men, allowed himself to be ousted from power by a mercenary leader, Heracleides, whom he later injudiciously pardoned for an act of treachery. Although he subsequently regained power and succeeded in expelling Dionysius' adherents from Ortygia, he was never able to put into effect the scheme of constitutional reform with which the letter credits him, and finally, after being forced to acquiesce in the murder of Heracleides, he was himself murdered in 354 by Callippus, a trusted Athenian friend who had accompanied him from Greece. His adherents sent to Plato an appeal for advice, to which the Seventh Letter purports to be an answer, and took refuge in the city of Leontini. Some months later Hipparinus, a son of Dionysius I by Dion's sister and a half-brother of Dionysius II, expelled Callippus from Syracuse and established himself in his place. The Eighth Letter belongs to the period between Hipparinus' adhesion to the cause of Dion's friends and his own downfall two years later at the hands of his brother Nysaeus. Nysaeus was in turn overthrown by Dionysius II, who had in the interval been ruling at Locri in southern Italy, but his restored tyranny proved so intolerable that finally in 345, two years after Plato's death, the Syracusans appealed to their mother city, Corinth, which sent a force under the able and upright Timoleon. He possessed the qualities which Dion lacked, and succeeded against all expectation in restoring peace and order in a country distracted by internal strife and threatened again by Carthaginian aggression. Dionysius, once more an exile, is said to have ended his life keeping a school at Corinth.

THE
SEVENTH AND EIGHTH
LETTERS

THE SEVENTH LETTER

*

The Seventh Letter is ostensibly a reply to a request for advice and help from Dion's adherents sent immediately after Dion's murder. Actually, however, it is an apologia for Plato's own career, and in particular for his intervention in Sicilian affairs, an open letter intended, like the letters of St Paul, for wide circulation.[1] The apologetic motive is explicitly mentioned more than once,[2] and it assorts queerly with the circumstances in which the letter purports to be written. One would not expect an appeal for advice at a moment of crisis to be answered by so long and elaborate a letter, which must have taken a considerable time to compose, which contains much that is not directly relevant to the needs of the moment, and which is quite clearly addressed to the world at large. It has been suggested either that the appeal for help is a 'literary device, introduced as a picturesque setting for the letter that follows',[3] or else that the apologia had been composed previously and was later fitted into the framework of a letter of advice.[4] Whatever view one takes of these suggestions, there is no escaping the fact that the structure of the letter is extremely odd, and many of the transitions between its parts abrupt and awkward.

After an introductory paragraph the letter begins with an autobiographical section describing Plato's early life and his reasons for abstaining from politics. It constitutes a self-revelation without which we should be almost entirely ignorant of Plato's personal development, and it has generally been accepted as historical. It ends with the famous statement that by 388 B.C., at the time of his first visit to Sicily, Plato had come to the conclusion that the only cure for the troubles of mankind lay in the combination of political power and philosophy in the same person, a conclusion identical with the proclama-

---

1. At the end of the first paragraph the genesis of Plato's political views is said to be 'worth the attention of both young and old'.

2. cf. 330C, 337E, 339A, and the final sentence of the letter (352A).

3. Harward, *The Platonic Epistles*, 1932, p. 190.

4. Post, *Thirteen Epistles of Plato*, 1925, p. 56.

tion of the need for philosopher-kings which is one of the central themes of the Republic.[1]

PLATO TO THE RELATIONS AND FRIENDS OF DION, GREETINGS

In your letter you tell me that I am to regard you as sharing the convictions that Dion held, and you urge me to co-operate with you in speech and action to the best of my ability. If your beliefs and aims are in fact the same as his I am ready to cooperate with you; otherwise I must give the matter further consideration. As for the nature of Dion's convictions and aims, I am in a position to give an account of them which is based on clear knowledge, not on guesswork. When I first came to Syracuse (I was then about forty) Dion was the same age as Hipparinus now,[2] and he acquired at that time and never abandoned to the day of his death a conviction that Syracuse must be free under the best government possible. So it would not be surprising if some divine providence led Hipparinus too to hold the same political creed. How that creed came into existence is a tale worth the attention of both young and old, and, seeing that this is an appropriate moment, I will try to relate it from the beginning.

When I was a young man I expected, like many others, to

---

1. *Republic* 473D, 499D.
2. Opinion is divided over the identity of Hipparinus. Two persons of the name are known, one a son of Dion, the other a son of Dionysius I by Dion's sister Aristomache and therefore a half-brother of Dionysius II. The latter joined with Dion's followers to overthrow Callippus (cf. p. 108), and it seems likelier that it is he who is meant here. The objection to this identification is that Hipparinus should not be much more than twenty in 353, if he is to be the same age as Dion was in 388, and that since his mother was married to Dionysius I about 398 this is improbable. It is not, however, impossible, and Plutarch (*Dion* 3) expressly says that Aristomache was childless for a long time after her marriage. If, on the other hand, Hipparinus is Dion's son, we are faced with the difficulty that, according to Plutarch (*Dion* 55), he died before his father. The difficulties about Hipparinus have been used as an argument against the authenticity of both the Seventh and Eighth Letters (see also pp. 151 f).

embark, as soon as I was my own master, on a political career. The condition in which I found public affairs was this. People were dissatisfied with the existing constitution, and a revolution took place, as a result of which power was concentrated in the hands of fifty-one men.[1] Eleven were in charge in the city and ten in Piraeus – each of these bodies had the supervision of the market and municipal affairs generally – while the remaining thirty assumed supreme control of the whole state. Some of them were relations and acquaintances of mine and invited me at once to join them in what seemed an obvious career for me. Naturally enough, in view of my youth, I expected that this government would bring about a change from corrupt to upright administration, and I watched with the keenest interest to see what they would do. I found that it had taken these men no time at all to make the previous government look like an age of gold; among other things they sent for Socrates, an older friend of mine, whom I would not hesitate to call the best man then living, and sent him with a number of others to arrest one of the citizens and bring him to execution. Their purpose in this was to involve Socrates in their actions, whether he liked it or not, but Socrates, so far from obeying, was prepared to risk everything rather than participate in their infamous deeds.[2] So when I saw all this and several other momentous events of the same sort I was disgusted and withdrew myself from the prevailing wickedness. Shortly afterwards a total revolution put an end to the rule of the Thirty, and once again, though more gradually, I began to feel a desire to take part in public life. Things were still unsettled, and even under the new government many things took place which one could not but condemn; it was not surprising that in a time of unrest some men seized the opportunity of taking an excessive revenge upon their enemies. Nevertheless the restored exiles behaved with great

325

---

1. Plato was born about 427 B.C. and the revolution which placed the Thirty in power took place in the summer of 404.

2. Socrates was sent with four others to arrest a certain Leon of Salamis, but ignored the order. cf. *Apology* 32C.

moderation. But it so happened that some men in power brought my associate Socrates before the courts on a wicked charge, to which Socrates least of all men should have been liable; they accused him of impiety, and the court condemned and put to death the man who, when the party now prevailing was outlawed and in exile, had refused to participate in the wrongful arrest of one of its own adherents.

So when I saw this and the kind of men who were active in politics and the principles on which things were managed, I concluded that it was difficult to take part in public life and retain one's integrity, and this feeling became stronger the more I observed and the older I became. Nothing could be done without friends and loyal associates. Such men were not easy to find among one's existing acquaintance, for affairs were no longer conducted on the principles practised by our ancestors, and new friends could not be acquired with any facility. Besides, the corruption of written law and established custom was proceeding at an astonishing rate, so that I, who began by being full of enthusiasm for a political career, ended by growing dizzy at the spectacle of universal confusion. I did not cease to consider how an improvement might be effected in this particular situation and in politics in general, and I remained on the watch for the right moment for action, but finally I came to the conclusion that the condition of all existing states is bad – nothing can cure their constitutions but a miraculous reform assisted by good luck – and I was driven to assert, in praise of true philosophy, that nothing else can enable one to see what is right for states and for individuals, and that the troubles of mankind will never cease until either true and genuine philosophers attain political power or the rulers of states by some dispensation of providence become genuine philosophers.

PLATO'S FIRST VISIT TO SICILY. HIS FRIENDSHIP WITH DION LEADS TO THE INVITATION TO VISIT DIONYSIUS II ON HIS ACCESSION TO POWER IN 367

What was the nature of the conversion which Dion with Plato's help hoped to effect in Dionysius? This is never clearly stated. At first sight, in view of the expectation attributed to Dion that now if ever there was chance of uniting the philosopher and the ruler in the same person, it is natural to suppose that they hoped to mould Dionysius into a philosopher-king of the type described in the Republic. *It seems likely, however, that the aim of Plato at any rate was much more modest. He states plainly that his advice to Dion's adherents is the same as that which was adopted by Dion and which he gave to Dionysius, and the three elements in this programme are the substitution for absolutism of constitutional government under the rule of law, the reformation of morals, and the resettlement of the devastated Greek cities and the protection of Greek Sicily from the Carthaginians. The emphasis on the importance of the rule of law, which shall be binding upon sovereigns and subjects alike, is fully in harmony with the view expressed by Plato in the late dialogue called the* Statesman (Politicus) *that a perfectly wise ruler who can dispense with constitutional restraints is an almost impossible ideal, and that a code of law is therefore indispensable. Similarly, the 'mixed' constitution recommended in the Eighth Letter finds its counterpart in the complex arrangements for a combination of oligarchy and democracy detailed in Plato's longest and latest work, the* Laws. *Nor is there good reason to think that, even at the time when he wrote the* Republic, *Plato believed in his philosopher-kings as a practical possibility. He may well have hoped that a change in Dionysius' outlook and way of life could result in constitutional reform,[1] but there is no need to attribute*

1. At *Laws* 709ff it is stated that a dictatorship provides the best basis for a change to good government, because of the reforms which a virtuous dictator has it in his power to make. It has been suggested that this was written with Dionysius in mind. On this whole subject cf. Morrow, G. R., *Plato's Epistles*, pp. 155ff.

to him the extreme political naïveté of expecting to found an ideal commonwealth in the conditions prevailing at Syracuse.

This was the state of mind in which I paid my first visit to Italy[1] and Sicily. When I arrived I found nothing whatever to please me in the tastes of a society devoted to Italian and Syracusan cookery,[2] where happiness was held to consist in filling oneself full twice a day, never sleeping alone at night, and indulging in the other pursuits that go with such a way of living. Brought up from boyhood in such an environment no man under heaven could become wise – he would need to be endowed with a temperament altogether miraculous – nor would he be any more likely to acquire self-control and the other qualities which go to make up goodness. Similarly no state, whatever its constitution, can enjoy peace and quietness if the citizens believe luxury to be the only proper object of expenditure and hold that men should be free from all other business to devote themselves entirely to feasting and drinking and the pursuit of love. Such a state must inevitably be involved in a never-ending round of revolution – it will be by turns a despotism, an oligarchy and a democracy – and those who hold power in it will not endure to hear a just and fair constitution so much as mentioned. With these thoughts in my head in addition to those which I have already spoken of, I made my way to Syracuse. Perhaps it was chance, but it looks as if some higher power was contriving at that time to lay the foundation of the events which have recently befallen Dion and Syracuse, and it may be of further events as well, unless you listen to the advice which I am now giving for the second time.[3] What do I mean by saying that my arrival in Sicily at that moment was the foundation of everything? Meeting

327

1. In Italy Plato first made the acquaintance of Archytas of Tarentum, the Pythagorean philosopher and statesman, who played a significant part in Plato's subsequent experiences in Sicily.

2. For Sicilian luxury cf. *Republic* 404C, *Gorgias* 518B.

3. The first time was presumably Plato's attempt to influence Dionysius II. Later (334D) he speaks of giving the same advice on three occasions, first to Dion, next to Dionysius, third, in this letter, to Dion's adherents.

Dion, who was then a young man, I disclosed to him in conversation the course which in my view is best for humanity and urged him to put it into practical effect; it looks as if by doing so I was in a sense unconsciously contriving the overthrow of despotism which was to take place. Dion at any rate, who was as quick to grasp my teaching as he was to grasp everything else, became a more enthusiastic convert to my views than any young man I have ever met, and resolved to spend the rest of his life very differently from the mass of Italians and Sicilians, adopting goodness as his ideal in preference to pleasure and luxury. So from that time to the death of the elder Dionysius he was something of a thorn in the flesh of those who were in the service of despotic government. When that event occurred he conceived the idea that he might not be alone in holding the views which true reasoning had led him to adopt; he observed them growing in the minds of others, not many, I admit, but some, and he believed that with the help of heaven the younger Dionysius might be one of them; his conversion, if it could be effected, would be an unspeakable blessing to the Syracusans in general as well as to Dionysius himself. Remembering how easily my association with him had converted him to a desire for the best and noblest way of life, he decided that I must at all costs return to Syracuse at once to take part in what was happening. If he were to succeed in his attempt to influence Dionysius he had high hopes that he could establish genuine happiness throughout the country without slaughter and bloodshed and the evils that have in fact occurred. Entertaining these ideas, as he was quite right to do, he persuaded Dionysius to send for me, and he added his own entreaties that I should come at once without fail, before others under whose influence Dionysius might fall should turn him from this ideal into less worthy courses. At the risk of being tedious I will transcribe his actual words. 'When', he asked, 'shall we get anything better than this heaven-sent opportunity?' Then he went on to tell at length of the empire established in Italy and Sicily, and of his own position in it, and of the youth and eagerness of Dionysius, 328 laying special emphasis on his aptitude for philosophy and education. He added that his own nephews and relations could easily be won over to the life and doctrine preached by me, and would be excellently placed to assist in converting Dionysius. So now, if ever, there was a possibility of realizing the hope of combining the philosopher and the ruler of a great state in the same person.

These, with many others of the same kind, were the arguments urged upon me by Dion. In coming to a decision I felt some fear how things would turn out with the younger men – young men are apt to fall a prey to sudden and often inconsistent impulses – but I knew that Dion was by nature serious-minded, and by this time he was already middle-aged. So, though I hesitated and debated whether I should accept the invitation and go, or how I should act, in the end what weighed with me was the consideration that, if ever an attempt was to be made to put into practice my convictions about law and government, now was the time; if I could persuade but one man fully to adopt my views I should have attained my whole object. Encouraged by these thoughts I set out from home. My motives were not what some supposed; what chiefly influenced me was fear of losing my self-respect and turning out in my own eyes a creature of mere words reluctant to embark upon any action, a traitor in the first place to the friendship and hospitality of Dion, who was actually in a position of no little danger. Suppose some disaster were to befall him, or suppose he were to be driven into exile by Dionysius and his other enemies and were to come to me as a fugitive and say: 'Plato, you see me here in exile, not for lack of infantry and cavalry to repel my enemies, but for want of convincing arguments, which I knew that you above all men were able to employ to convert young men to goodness and righteousness, and to establish love and friendship between them whatever the circumstances. It is because you have done nothing to supply my want of such arguments that I have left Syracuse and am here. And *my* plight is the lesser part of the disgrace that you have incurred; can you deny that on this occasion you have by betraying me betrayed philosophy itself, which you are always praising and which you assert that the rest of the world treats with dishonour? If I were an inhabitant of Megara,[1] you could not refuse to come in answer to my appeals for help without entirely forfeiting your self-respect. Do you suppose for a moment that, as things are, you can escape the reputation of cowardice by excusing yourself on the score of the length of the journey and the hardships involved in so great a voyage? Quite the contrary.' What plausible answer could I make to such an indictment? None. So I decided to obey the claims of reason and justice as far as is humanly possible, and went; these were the motives which led me to abandon my normal pursuits, which are far from discreditable, and live under a despotism which seemed inconsistent with my convictions and my character. By so doing I discharged the claims of hospitality and preserved myself from any reproach from philosophy, which would have suffered shame if I had played the coward and incurred disgrace by shirking my duty.

When I arrived – to cut short a long story – I found the court of Dionysius seething with intrigue, and Dion the object of much misrepresentation to the authorities. I defended him to the best of my ability, but that ability was small, and about four months after my arrival Dionysius accused Dion of plotting against the government, put him aboard a small ship, and sent him into exile. After that all of us who were friends of Dion feared that Dionysius would fasten on one of us an accusation of being Dion's accomplice; there was even a rumour in Syracuse about me that I had been put to death by Dionysius for being the prime cause of the whole business. But Dionysius, seeing our state of mind and fearing that our apprehensions might give rise to something worse, tried to win us all over by cordiality; me in particular he set himself to console and encourage, and begged me by all means to stay; his credit was involved in my staying rather than

1. The point is that Megara, a town on the isthmus of Corinth, was only a short distance from Athens.

running away from him, and for this reason he pretended to be very much in earnest in his requests, though we know of course that the requests of despots have an element of compulsion about them. In pursuit of his end and to prevent my departure he brought and lodged me inside the citadel, from which no ship's captain would have dared to remove me without an express order to this effect sent by Dionysius himself, still less in defiance of Dionysius' prohibition. Nor would any merchant or any officer in command at the frontier have allowed me to leave the country on my own; he would have arrested me and taken me straight back to Dionysius, especially as it was now being rumoured, contrary to the earlier report, that Dionysius was wonderfully fond of Plato. What was the real situation? The truth of the matter is that as time went on and he became more familiar with my character and way of life Dionysius did in fact become fonder of me; but he wanted to supplant Dion in my esteem and to take his place as my particular friend, and he showed wonderful eagerness in his efforts to achieve this. He shrank, however, from the best method of gaining his end, if it could be gained at all, which was to make himself my pupil and take part with me in philosophical discussion; our ill-wishers had made him fear that if he did that he would find himself in a trap, and that Dion would thus have accomplished his whole aim. I put up with all this, adhering to the original purpose of my visit, in the hope that he might somehow come to desire the life of philosophy, but his resistance was too much for me.

ADVICE TO THE ADHERENTS OF DION

Plato now turns to what he professes to regard as the main purpose of his letter, advice to Dion's party. The main points in this have been mentioned in the preface to the previous section; they are introduced here in a somewhat discursive manner and with a good deal of repetitiveness, and they are said to constitute the same policy as Dion and Plato urged upon Dionysius and as Dion would himself have attempted to put into effect had he lived. Great stress is laid on the importance of self-discipline in those in power, and on the necessity of establishing a code of law. For the latter Plato's correspondents are urged to seek the help of wise men from other parts of the Greek world, and to entrust them with the task of legislating for Syracuse. There is nothing foreign to Greek sentiment in such a suggestion. Plutarch (Dion 53) says that before his death Dion had sent for advisers from Corinth, the mother city of Syracuse, and we hear of many prominent members of the Academy being sent on legislative missions. The number, however, of the advisers suggested seems unrealistic (cf. p. 130, n. 1).

It is to be noticed that the advice which this section contains is interwoven with other material, much of it apologetic in purpose. This is particularly true of the paragraph in which Plato exonerates Athens from any blame for the treachery of the Athenian Callippus. Here he is explicitly answering a definite charge. But a similar purpose is to be seen also in the emphasis with which Plato deprecates interference in politics unasked or where nothing can be achieved without the use of force. It is surely natural to see here a justification for his own abstention from Athenian politics.

These are the reasons which account for my first visit to Sicily and the time that I spent there. Later on I left home again and returned once more to Sicily at the urgent behest of Dionysius. But before I give my reasons for doing so and attempt to explain and justify what I did for the benefit of those who are always asking me what was my motive in going a second time, I will first advise you on your best course in the present circumstances; otherwise I shall be treating as my main theme what is really a side issue. What I have to say is this.

When a man is sick and following a course injurious to his health, surely the first task of anyone whom he consults must be to change his way of life, and make sure of his willingness to obey instructions before going on to give more detailed advice. If he is not willing, a genuine physician who is a man of spirit will, in my opinion, avoid further consultation; to continue to advise in these circumstances indicates a lack both of spirit and of skill. The same is true of a state, whether its government is in the hands of one man or of many; when its government is on the right lines a sensible man will give advice if he is consulted on any matter touching its interests. But if those who consult him have completely abandoned the true principles of government and firmly refuse to return to the right track, and tell their adviser to let the constitution alone on pain of death and to confine himself to advising on the quickest and easiest way for them to obtain the permanent satisfaction of their wishes and desires, I should call the person who gave advice on these terms a coward and the person who refused it a brave man. This is my conviction, and, whenever someone consults me on a matter of importance in his own life, his property, for example, or his physical or spiritual well-being, I first consider whether his daily life is directed by any principle and whether he is willing to listen to my advice on the subject communicated to me. If he is I am delighted to advise him, and there is nothing perfunctory about my treatment of his problem. But if I am not consulted at all, or if it is perfectly clear that my advice will not be taken, I do not come forward with it unasked; as for compulsion, I would not exercise it even on my own son. I might offer advice to a slave, or even compel him if he were recalcitrant, but to put compulsion on one's father or mother I do not think right, unless they should be suffering from some mental derangement.[1] If they have a settled way of life which pleases them, though it may not please me, it is not for me either to make enemies of them by useless admonitions or to pander to them by helping them to obtain the satisfaction of desires which I myself would rather die than entertain. The same principle will be followed by a wise man in his behaviour towards his own state; if he thinks anything amiss with its government he will speak out, provided that his words are not going to be wasted or to bring him to his death, but he will not attempt to change the constitution of his native land by force. When reformation cannot be achieved without the infliction of exile and death on

331

1. cf. *Crito* 51C. 'It is not right to put compulsion on one's father or mother, and still less on one's country.'

some people, he will simply keep quiet and pray for the welfare of himself and his country.[1]

Acting on this principle I would give the same advice to
you as I joined with Dion in giving to Dionysius. This was in
the first place to conduct his daily life on such a plan as to give
him the highest possible degree of mastery over himself and
to win him loyal friends and associates. In this way he would
avoid the fate of his father, who, when he came into possession of many cities which had been completely sacked by the
barbarians, was unable to resettle them by establishing in each
a loyal government managed by friends; he could not find   332
such people either among foreigners or among his younger
brothers, though he had brought up the latter himself, and
raised them from a private station to positions of power and
from poverty to exceptional wealth. Neither persuasion nor
teaching, neither favours nor ties of blood, enabled him to
make any of them the partners of his rule; he was seven times
worse off than Darius,[2] who, though he had no brothers or
men brought up by himself to depend on, but only those who
had helped him to overthrow the Mede and the Eunuch,
divided his realm among them in seven parts, each larger than
the whole of Sicily, and found that he could rely on the
loyalty of partners who attacked neither him nor one another.
Darius set an example of what a good law-giver and king
should be; he established laws which have preserved the
Persian empire to the present day. The same may be said of
the Athenians, who took over a number of Greek cities which

1. cf. *Republic* 496, where the philosopher is advised to keep quiet like
a man sheltering from a storm under a wall.

2. Darius became king of Persia by destroying a Median usurper
called Smerdis with the aid of *six* confederates. For the whole story cf.
Herodotus 3. 61ff. According to Herodotus Darius divided his realm into
twenty satrapies. An inscription at Persepolis gives the number as
twenty-four. These discrepancies have been used as an argument against
the authenticity of the letter. But Plato follows the same version in *Laws*
695c, where the number of provinces is again given as *seven* and the
pretender called the Eunuch.

had been invaded by the barbarians[1] but were still inhabited. Though they had not founded them themselves they preserved their empire over them for seventy years by having in each of them men in power who were their friends. But Dionysius, though he united the whole of Sicily into one state, because he was too shrewd to trust anyone hardly managed to survive. He was poor in loyal and true friends, and a man's possession or lack of these is the surest indication of a good or bad disposition.

This is the advice that Dion and I gave to Dionysius, seeing that his father's neglect had left him devoid of education and of suitable society. We urged him first of all to reform his own life,[2] next, when he had started on this course, to find among his kinsmen and contemporaries friends who would be of like mind with himself in the pursuit of goodness, and above all to be consistent in his own conduct, for in this respect he had grown up remarkably deficient. We did not use such plain language as this – it was not safe to do so – but we succeeded by veiled allusions in maintaining the thesis that every man who would preserve himself and the people he rules must follow this course, and that any other will lead to utter destruction. If he would take the way which we pointed out to him and make himself into an intelligent and disciplined person he might resettle the deserted cities of Sicily and bind them together by such political institutions as would dispose them to come to his aid and one another's against attacks by the barbarians;[3] in this way he would have an empire not merely double his father's but in reality many times as great. For if all this came to pass he would be in a position to impose upon the Carthaginians a yoke far heavier than they endured in the time of Gelon[4] instead of continuing to pay tribute to them under the agreement made by his father.

333

1. i.e. the Persians. The Athenian empire lasted for approximately seventy years ending in 404 B.C.
2. I follow Burnet in assuming a lacuna after πρῶτον.
3. In this case the Carthaginians.
4. Gelon, tyrant of Syracuse, defeated the Syracusans at Himera in 480 B.C. and exacted an indemnity from them.

These were the exhortations addressed to Dionysius by us, who, according to the reports current in many quarters, were plotting against him. These reports obtained such credit with Dionysius that they brought about the banishment of Dion, and threw us into a state of fear. To come at once to the end of the many events which happened in a brief space, Dion returned from the Peloponnese and Athens and taught Dionysius a lesson which was far from theoretical. But, when he had twice[1] freed their city and restored it to them, the Syracusans exhibited the same feelings towards Dion as had Dionysius. Dion's attempt to make himself a partner in the whole of Dionysius' life was made in the belief that he could educate him and mould him into a monarch worthy of his throne, but Dionysius preferred to side with Dion's enemies, who declared that everything that Dion did at that period was part of a plot against the despotic government, and that his aim in educating Dionysius was to bewitch him into neglecting his royal office and entrusting it to Dion, who would then make it his own and treacherously deprive Dionysius of his throne. These were the slanders which won the day then, and afterwards a second time, when they were circulated in Syracuse; and very monstrous this victory was and shameful to those who were the authors of it. Its exact nature must be made plain to those who are asking me to intervene in the present situation.

I, an Athenian citizen and an associate of Dion, went to the court of the despot to help in establishing friendship between Dionysius and Dion instead of hostility, but in my struggle with those who were making trouble I was worsted. Dionysius tried by honours and gifts to win me over to his side, and to persuade me to testify that he was justified in banishing Dion, but he entirely failed. At a later period Dion returned home, bringing in his train two brothers from Athens,[2]

1. First, when he took the city from Dionysius II on his arrival from Greece, second, when he was recalled from Leontini to protect it against Nypsius, Dionysius' lieutenant.
2. Callippus and Philostratus. cf. Plutarch, *Dion* 54.

whose friendship he had acquired not through philosophy but by the sort of chance acquaintance which forms the basis of most friendships, and which is exercised in mutual hospitality and participation in the rites and ceremonies of the mysteries; it was in this way and because of the services they rendered in connection with his return that these two became Dion's associates. When they arrived in Sicily and found that false reports of Dion's ambition to make himself dictator were being spread among the very Sicilians whom he had liberated, they not only betrayed the friend whose hospitality they had enjoyed but may almost be said to have murdered him with their own hands, inasmuch as they stood by fully armed to help his assassins. The foulness and wickedness of this act calls for no comment from me – many others both now and hereafter will make it their business to sing in that strain. There is however one point that I cannot pass over. It is commonly said that the name of Athens is dishonoured by the conduct of these men. But I could point out that the man who refused to betray this same Dion, when by doing so he might have acquired great wealth and honour, is also an Athenian. His friendship with Dion was based not on vulgar good-fellowship but on association in liberal studies, and this, rather than spiritual[1] or physical kinship, is the only sure foundation of friendship for a man of sense. So I maintain that the reputation of Athens cannot fairly be held to have been stained by Dion's murderers: to think otherwise is to ascribe to them an importance which they never possessed.

All that I have been saying is for the benefit of Dion's relations and friends, but to it I have to add the same advice and the same teaching as I have already given twice before to two other hearers. The substance of that teaching is that Sicily, like other states, should be subject not to the tyranny of men but to the rule of law. Absolute power is bad both for those who exercise it and for those who are subject to it, for themselves and their children's children and their remoter

1. Presumably referring to the bond formed by initiation into the mysteries.

descendants; the experience of it is utter destruction, and the prizes which it confers are snatched at only by small and mean souls, who know nothing of what is good and right both here and hereafter, both in earth and heaven. This is the truth which I preached first to Dion, then to Dionysius, and now for the third time I am preaching to you. Listen to me then for the sake of Zeus the Saviour, to whom the third libation belongs,[1] and consider also the destinies of Dionysius and Dion. Dionysius rejected my teaching and though he is still alive lives in dishonour: Dion embraced it and died a glorious death; for to meet whatever fate sends in the attempt to reach the highest for oneself and one's country is altogether right and glorious. None of us is exempt from death, nor if he were would he be happy, as men commonly suppose; good and evil are meaningless to things that have no soul; it is only a soul either in the body or separated from it which can experience either. Now we must always hold fast to the sacred truth declared of old that the soul is immortal, and when it is separated from the body must submit to judgement and be severely punished; that is why we must believe it a lesser evil to suffer even great wrongs and injuries than to inflict them. But this is something to which the man whose greed for wealth matches the poverty of his soul pays no heed, or if he does he supposes that he can afford to mock at it, while he snatches shamelessly, like an animal, at whatever he thinks will enable him to satisfy his appetite for food or drink or for that coarse and shameless pleasure which wrongly takes its name from Aphrodite. He is blind and does not see the consequences entailed by his abominable acts of rapacity, and how each wicked deed increases the burden of evil which the wrongdoer must drag about with him, not only while he wanders upon the earth but when he has taken his utterly shameful and miserable journey back to the world below.

These and such as these were the convictions which I tried to impress upon Dion, and I have as good cause to be angry

335

1. A reference to the custom at banquets where the third and last libation was poured to Zeus the Saviour.

with his murderers as with Dionysius. Both parties have
inflicted upon me and, I may say, upon the world at large a
wrong of the gravest kind, the first by destroying the man who
wished to put justice into effect, the second by refusing to put
justice into effect throughout his realm though he had the
power to do so. If he had really united philosophy and political
power in the same person he might have given a light to the
whole world, Greek and barbarian alike, and brought home
to everybody the truth that neither a state nor an individual
can be happy whose life is not lived wisely under the guidance
of justice, an ideal which requires either that a man should
possess these virtues in himself or else that he should have
been bred and trained in the ways of righteousness under the
rule of men of holiness. This is the wrong perpetrated by
Dionysius, and the other injuries that I suffered from him are
trivial in comparison. But the murderer of Dion has un-
wittingly produced the same effect. I know for certain, in so
far as one human being can speak with certainty of another,
that if Dion had become master of the state the form which
his rule would have taken would have been this. First of all,
once he had freed his native Syracuse from the yoke of slavery
and washed away her stains and dressed her in the garb of
liberty, he would have spared no pains to equip her citizens
with a fitting system of law based on the best principles. Next,
he would have set eagerly about the business of resettling the
whole of Sicily and freeing it from the barbarians, expelling
some of them and subjugating the rest, a task in which he
would have met with fewer obstacles than Hiero.[1] Now, if this
had been effected by a man who, besides being brave and upright and disciplined, was a philosopher, the masses would
have acquired the same respect for goodness as would have
arisen among mankind at large and proved its salvation, if I
had succeeded in convincing Dionysius. But as things have
turned out some evil spirit has attacked us, bringing with it
contempt for law and religion and, worst of all, the reckless-

1. The brother of Gelon and his successor at Syracuse.

ness of ignorance – a soil in which all evil things take root and grow and produce in the end a crop most bitter to those who sowed it. It has overturned and ruined all our plans for the second time. Let us not however say anything which might bring bad luck upon a third attempt.

In spite of all that has happened, I advise you who were Dion's friends to imitate his love for his country and the simplicity of his style of living, and to try to realize his aims under better auspices. What those aims were I have already explained quite clearly. But if any of you is unable to live in the old Doric way like your fathers, and hankers after the Sicilian fashions followed by the murderers of Dion, do not enlist his aid or suppose him capable of acting reliably and in good faith. Otherwise, for the task of resettling the whole of Sicily so that all shall enjoy equal rights, call to your help men from all over the Peloponnese as well as from Sicily itself, and do not fear to approach even Athens; there too you will find men of pre-eminent excellence who hate the hardened audacity of such as kill their host. But if this must be deferred to a later stage, because you are hard pressed by the internal strife which springs up daily among you in many different forms, then anyone to whom providence has granted even a modicum of right belief must realize that the horrors of civil war will never come to an end until those who have gained the upper hand cease to seek for the satisfaction of old grudges by pitched battles or by banishing and slaughtering their opponents, and abandon the idea of punishing their enemies. Instead of this they must restrain themselves and, having established for the common good a system of law as much to the advantage of the vanquished as of themselves, compel their former foes to be law-abiding by the operation of the twin motives of shame and fear – fear, because the winners have shown that they have a superiority of force, and shame, because they are clearly better at controlling their desires, and more able as well as more willing to subject themselves to the law. This is the only way in which a state torn by civil war can bring its troubles to an end; otherwise such states are liable to be for ever

337

divided against themselves by strife and enmity, hatred and distrust.

The victors then at any particular moment, if they wish to achieve security, must choose out after mutual consultation the best men that they can find among the Greeks, men of advanced age in the first place who have wives and children at home, and who can trace their descent from a long and honourable line of distinguished ancestors and each possess an adequate amount of property. For a city with a population of ten thousand fifty such will be a sufficient number.[1] These men must be induced by earnest entreaties and by the offer of the highest honours to leave their homes, and on their arrival requested and required to frame a code of law, first binding themselves by an oath to show no favour either to winners or to losers but to act impartially in the interest of the city as a whole. Once the law has been framed everything will depend on the winning side showing itself more ready to obey the law than the losers; if it does so all will be well; security and prosperity will prevail, and the state will be delivered from all its troubles. But in the opposite event do not call on me or anyone else for help in dealing with those who will not abide by the principles I have laid down. This course is akin to that which Dion and I tried jointly to put into effect for the good of Syracuse. It is however only second best. The best is that which we hoped to carry through with the cooperation of Dionysius himself,[2] but fate which is stronger than men brought our plans to naught. So now it is for you to try to bring things to a happier outcome, and may heaven send you good fortune and success in the attempt.

1. It has been suggested that this sentence is a later insertion. The number seems much too large, and there seems no point in its being proportional to the population. In the Eighth Letter (356C) the number of such a committee is left to be settled by agreement, and in Laws (704C) a similar committee has only ten members.

2. Omitting the words πᾶσιν κοινὰ ἀγαβά, 'goods common to all', as a gloss, inserted by a scribe who supposed that the best course was the communism advocated for philosopher-kings in the Republic. There is no suggestion elsewhere that such a course was ever urged upon Dionysius. cf. Morrow, Plato's Epistles, pp. 160ff.

PLATO'S SECOND VISIT TO DIONYSIUS II

Plato is at pains to emphasize the reluctance with which he embarked on his last visit to Syracuse. Ultimately he decided to go, partly to do what he could to protect Dion's interests, partly because Archytas and other Pythagorean friends represented to him that Dionysius' interest in philosophy was far from extinct. A further motive which is implied rather than explicitly stated was probably to protect his own philosophical reputation. The news that Dionysius was engaged in philosophical discussion must have raised doubts in the mind of Plato, who knew how slight was Dionysius' acquaintance with Platonic thought. After the visit, which confirmed Plato's fears, Dionysius appears to have written a book on Plato's philosophy which Plato repudiates in the strongest terms. It leads him to declare that no written exposition of his fundamental thought is possible or desirable, and that he himself has never written and will never write a treatise about it. The only way in which it can be learned is by long association between teacher and pupil, and the depreciation of writing repeats in stronger terms the view of the matter put forward in the Phaedrus *275ff (pp. 97ff above).*

In view of Plato's own extensive writings the denial that he has written or will write is strange. It has to be remembered, however, that his own writings are dialogues, not systematic treatises, and that none of them contains a formal exposition of the Theory of Forms. In the Republic *(506ff) Socrates declares that the supreme idea of good can be conveyed only by an analogy, that of the sun, and both there and elsewhere Plato speaks of the ultimate apprehension of the good as something in the nature of a mystical experience, which is incommunicable. Very much the same language is used in this letter. In addition, Aristotle, who in one passage speaks of 'Plato's unwritten opinions',[1] provides strong grounds for thinking that in their latest form Plato's views on metaphysics became increasingly mathematical, and developed considerably beyond anything found in the dialogues. There is a tradition also of a lecture on the good which its hearers found so mathematical as to be unintelligible.[2]*

---

1. *Physics* 209B, 15.
2. Aristoxenus, *Harmonics* 30–31. Aristoxenus was a pupil of Aristotle, and says that Aristotle used to tell this story.

So much then for the advice I have to send you, and for the story of my first visit to Dionysius. As for my later journey overseas, anyone who is interested may learn from what follows how naturally and reasonably that came about. My first stay was spent as I described earlier, before formulating my advice to the friends and relatives of Dion. I used every means in my power to persuade Dionysius to let me go, and at last we came to an agreement. Dionysius undertook to send for Dion and me again when the war which was then going on in Sicily came to an end, and when he had put his rule on a more secure footing. In the meantime he asked Dion to regard his present position as a change of residence rather than exile, and on these terms I promised that I would return. When peace was restored Dionysius sent for me, but asked Dion to remain abroad for another year; he was, however, most anxious that I should come. Dion urged and begged me to go, because reports were constantly coming from Sicily that Dionysius was once more wonderfully enamoured of philosophy; for this reason Dion besought me most earnestly not to refuse the invitation. I knew that philosophy often has this sort of effect on young men; nevertheless I judged it safer for the moment to leave both Dion and Dionysius severely alone, and I made myself unpopular with both of them by answering that I was an old man and that what was now happening was totally incompatible with our previous agreement.

Next, it appears, Archytas[1] paid a visit to Dionysius; for before I left Sicily I had established ties of hospitality and friendship between Archytas and his school at Tarentum and Dionysius. There were others too at Syracuse who had received some instruction from Dion, and others again to whom they had in turn imparted it. Full of second-hand philosophical notions these people were apparently trying to converse with Dionysius about them as if he were thoroughly acquainted with all my views. Now Dionysius, besides having a certain aptitude for study, is wonderfully keen to excel; so

1. For Archytas of Tarentum, cf. p. 116, n. 1.

he was probably pleased to be addressed in this way and
ashamed to let it become known that he had learnt nothing
when I was at his court. The result was that he conceived a
desire to get a clearer light on these matters and was at the
same time driven on by a wish not to be outdone. The reason
why he learnt nothing during my previous visit I have
explained in what I have already written. So when I was
safely home and, as I said just now, refused his second
invitation, Dionysius, I suppose, felt passionately that his
honour was involved in not having it thought that I had a
poor opinion of his nature and character, and that after
becoming acquainted with his way of living I was too disgusted
to be still willing to visit him.

339

Now I am bound to tell the truth, and I must put up with it
if anyone who hears what happened despises my philosophy
and applauds the despot's intelligence. At his third attempt
Dionysius sent a trireme for me to make my journey easier,
and with it came Archedemus and some other Sicilian
acquaintances of mine. He sent Archedemus, one of the
disciples of Archytas, because he believed that I thought more
highly of him than of anyone else in Sicily. All these brought
me the same report, that Dionysius had made remarkable
progress in philosophy. He also sent me a very long letter,
knowing my affection for Dion and how eager Dion was that
I should make the voyage and return to Syracuse. The letter
was composed with an eye to all this, and its beginning ran
more or less as follows. After the usual form of address and
the conventional greeting, without any further preliminary it
went on like this: 'If you now return to Sicily at my invitation,
I assure you in the first place that Dion's affairs shall be
settled to your satisfaction; I am sure that your wishes will be
reasonable, and I will fall in with them. But if you refuse you
will find that nothing which concerns Dion either personally
or in any other way will turn out to your liking.' That is what
the letter said; to repeat the rest of it would take too long and
would not be to the point. Other letters too came to me from
Archytas and the group at Tarentum, which spoke highly of

Dionysius' progress in philosophy, and added that if I did not come at once I should utterly undo the friendship which I had established between them and Dionysius, a friendship which was of no small importance to them politically. So when Dionysius' summons took this form, and I found that on one side I was being pulled by my friends in Sicily and Italy, while on the other those at Athens were positively pushing me out of the country with their importunity, I was confronted by the same argument as before, that I must not betray Dion and my friends and associates at Tarentum. In addition to this it occurred to me that there was nothing surprising in a young man of good natural ability, who had heard serious subjects talked of, conceiving a passionate desire for the best way of life. It was my duty therefore to make such inquiries as would settle the matter one way or the other; I must not shirk this duty and incur the reproach which would genuinely be mine if the reports that had come to me were really true.

340   So, under cover of this reasoning, I set out, full of apprehension and expecting, as you may easily suppose, no very happy outcome. My journey, however, had at least this result that I discovered for myself the truth of the saying 'third time lucky', for I had the good fortune to come safe home again. For this after God I have to thank Dionysius, who frustrated the attempts of a number of people to destroy me, and showed in his dealings with me that he was not altogether devoid of shame.

When I arrived I made it my first task to discover whether Dionysius was genuinely on fire with enthusiasm for philosophy or whether the frequent reports to this effect which had come to Athens were baseless. There is a way of testing this which involves no loss of dignity and is quite suitable for absolute rulers, especially such as are full of second-hand ideas, which I perceived as soon as I arrived to be very much the case with Dionysius. The method is to demonstrate to such people the nature of the subject as a whole, and all the stages that must be gone through, and how much labour is required. If the hearer has the divine spark which makes philosophy congenial to him and fits him for its pursuit, the way described to him appears so wonderful that he must follow it with all his might if life is to be worth living. So from that moment he puts pressure both on himself and on his guide, never letting him go until he either reaches his final goal or is able to make his own way for himself without the aid of his mentor. This is the state of mind in which such a man lives, discharging whatever business he may be engaged in, but holding fast throughout to philosophy and to the daily routine which will do most to foster his powers of learning and remembering and conducting sober debate within his own mind; for the opposite course he conceives a hatred which lasts till he dies.

But those who are not genuinely lovers of wisdom, in whom philosophy is no more than a superficial veneer like the tan men get by exposing themselves to the sun, once they see how much there is to learn and the labour involved and the disciplined way of life that the subject requires, decide that the task is too hard for them and beyond their scope. They are not in fact fit to practise philosophy, though some of them persuade themselves that they have a sufficient grasp of the whole matter and need give themselves no further trouble about it. This then is the clearest and safest test to apply to those who like soft living and are incapable of hard work; it has the advantage that a man has only himself to blame if he cannot meet the demands of the subject, and his guide is absolved from responsibility.

It was with this in mind that I said what I did to Dionysius. I did not give him a complete exposition, nor did he ask me for one; he pretended that what he had heard from other people had already given him an adequate knowledge of many of the most important parts of the subject. I am told that since then he has written a book about what he learnt at that time, putting it together as if it were a treatise of his own, quite different from what I taught him; but of this I know nothing. I know that some others have also written on the same topics, but such men are ignorant even of themselves.[1] But this much at any rate I can affirm about any present or future writers who pretend to knowledge of the matters with which I concern myself, whether they claim to have been taught by me or by a third party or to have discovered the truth for themselves; in my judgement it is impossible that they should have any understanding of the subject. No treatise by me concerning it exists or ever will exist. It is not something that can be put into words like other branches of learning; only after long partnership in a common life devoted to this very thing does truth flash upon the soul, like a flame kindled by a leaping spark, and once it is born there it nourishes itself thereafter. Yet this too I know, that if there were to be any oral or written teaching on this matter it would best come from me, and that it is I who would feel most deeply the harm caused by an inferior exposition. If I thought that any adequate spoken or written account could be given to the world at large, what more glorious life-work could I have undertaken than to put into writing what would be of great benefit to mankind and to bring the nature of reality to light for all to see? But I do not think that the attempt to put these matters into words would be to men's advantage, except to those few who can find out the truth for themselves with a little guidance; the rest would be filled either with an un-justifiable and quite improper contempt for their fellows or with a lofty and vain expectation, based on the belief that they were in possession of some mighty secret.

THE INADEQUACY OF WORDS TO EXPRESS
THE NATURE OF REALITY

The notoriously difficult metaphysical digression which follows has been much discussed. Some even of those who regard the rest of the letter as authentic have dismissed it as an irrelevant interpolation;

1. The meaning of the Greek is obscure. There may however be a reference to the importance of self-knowledge as a necessary basis for any advance in philosophy and to the Delphic maxim 'Know thyself'. cf. *Phaedrus* 229E (p. 25 above).

others have treated it not only as a necessary part of the writer's argument but as a passage of great importance for the understanding of Plato's thought. For a good brief exposition of its meaning cf. W. D. Ross, Plato's Theory of Ideas (Oxford, 1951), pp. 139–141. Ross holds that 'the passage indicates, more clearly perhaps than any other in Plato, his sense of the difficulties which attend the search for knowledge of the Ideas.'

Two points of particular interest may be noted. First, though the passage contains (342D) what Ross calls 'the most catholic list of types of idea to be found anywhere in Plato', neither of the two names which Plato uses elsewhere for the Forms (idea and eidos) is used at all. Second, at 342C knowledge (episteme), understanding (nous), and true opinion (doxa) are classed together, in contrast with the sharp distinction which Plato usually draws between the first two and the last. This point has been much stressed by opponents of the authenticity of the passage. It should, however, be observed that the writer adds that understanding has a nearer affinity to reality than the other two.

On this point I have it in mind to speak at greater length, because it may be that my meaning will be clearer when I have done so. There is a true argument which stands in the way of anyone who dares to write anything whatever on such matters. It has often been used by me in the past, but it needs to be stated again on this occasion.

For everything that exists we may distinguish three instruments by which knowledge of it must be acquired; knowledge itself is a fourth member of the group, and the actual entity which is the object of knowledge and truly exists must be regarded as a fifth. There is then, first, the name, second, the definition, third, the representation, and fourth, knowledge.[1] Take[2] a single example if you wish to understand my

---

1. At *Laws* 895D three things are said to be involved in knowing any object: the object itself, its definition, and its name. The reality there discussed is soul, and mention of a 'representation' would not be appropriate, as it is here where the example chosen is the circle, which can be represented by a diagram.

2. The use of the imperative singular in this sentence has been taken to suggest that the writer is incorporating matter used in another context.

meaning, and then apply that understanding universally. There is an object called 'circle'. Its name is the word that I have just uttered. Next comes its definition, compounded of nouns and verbs; for the object named 'round' and 'circumference' and 'circle' the definition would be 'the thing whose extremities in every direction are equidistant from its centre'. Third, there is the representation, which can be drawn and rubbed out or turned on a lathe and later destroyed; none of these things can happen to the real circle, to which all these three refer, because it is something quite different from them. Fourth, there is knowledge and understanding and true belief about these things; these must be classed together, because they reside not in sounds or in physical shapes but in souls; clearly then they must be distinguished both from the real circle itself and from the three instruments first mentioned. Of these understanding comes closest to the fifth in kinship and likeness and the others are more distant.

The same holds good of straight as of curved shapes and surfaces, of goodness, beauty and justice, of all physical bodies natural or artificial, of fire, water and the other elements, of all living beings and moral qualities, and of all the things that men do or have done to them; in every case, unless a man somehow grasps the first four, he will never attain perfect knowledge of the fifth. Moreover, owing to the inadequacy of language, these four are as much concerned to demonstrate what any particular thing is like as to reveal its essential being; that is why no intelligent man will ever dare to commit his thoughts to words, still less to words that cannot be changed, as is the case with what is expressed in written characters.[1]

What has just been said, however, requires further explanation. Every circle that is drawn or turned on a lathe is full in practice of the opposite of the reality to which we have assigned the fifth place. At every point it is in contact with the straight, whereas the circle itself, I maintain, has in it no

1. cf. *Phaedrus* 275D.

element, small or great, of the nature which is its opposite.[1] Besides, none of these things has a name that we can regard as fixed. There is nothing to stop the things which are at present called 'round' being called 'straight' and vice versa, and their stability would be in no way impaired if one made this transposition and called them by the opposite names. The same is true of the definition; being compounded of nouns and verbs it is in consequence far from being adequately stable. One might employ innumerable arguments to demonstrate the inaccuracy of each of the four, but the most powerful is this. There are, as I said just now, two things which must be distinguished; what a thing is like and its essential being. Now the soul is searching for knowledge of essential being, but what each of the four offers it, whether in words or in actual practice, is not what it is searching for, but something which, whether it is expressed in words or displayed in visible form, can be easily refuted by the evidence of the senses; the result is to create perplexity and obscurity in practically every man's mind. When we are dealing with matters on which, owing to our bad training, we are not in the habit of searching for the truth, but are satisfied to accept what is offered to us as representations of it, we do not make ourselves mutually ridiculous when we ask and answer questions based on an ability to manipulate and criticize the four instruments; but when it is a matter of requiring a clear demonstration of the essential being which occupies the fifth place, anyone who has mastered the art of refutation gains the day, and makes the expositor of a doctrine, whether he is speaking or writing or answering questions, appear in the eyes of his audience totally ignorant of the subject on which he is attempting to write or speak. It may sometimes happen that the audience is unaware that it is not the soul of the writer or speaker which is at fault, but the four instruments

1. The meaning is that any tangent drawn to a circle physically described will coincide with it for a certain distance. No concrete representation of a circle is absolutely circular.

that I have enumerated, each of which is by its very nature defective.

It is only by the constant use of all four instruments, moving up and down from one to another, that knowledge of what is in its nature good can be engendered – and that with difficulty – in a soul which is itself naturally good. Where the soul is ill-endowed, as most souls are both intellectually and morally – in some cases too a good endowment has been spoilt – Lynceus himself could not make a man see.[1] To put it in a word, neither facility in learning nor a good memory can make a man see if his nature is not akin to the object; such knowledge simply cannot come to birth in constitutions which are alien to it. Those then who have no natural affinity or kinship with justice and other forms of excellence, however quick and retentive they may be in other matters, and those in whom a natural affinity is accompanied by slowness of apprehension and forgetfulness, can none of them acquire such knowledge as is attainable about virtue and vice.[2] I add vice, because both of them must be learnt together, and this requires great expense of time and trouble, as I began by saying. It is only when all these things, names and definitions, visual and other sensations, are rubbed together and subjected to tests in which questions and answers are exchanged in good faith and without malice that finally, when human capacity is stretched to its limit, a spark of understanding and intelligence flashes out and illuminates the subject at issue.[3] That is why any serious student of serious realities will shrink from making truth the helpless object of men's ill-will by committing it to writing. In a word, the conclusion to be drawn is this; when one sees a written composition, whether it be on law by a legislator or on any other subject, one can be sure, if the

1. Lynceus, one of the Argonauts, was proverbially keen-sighted.

2. For the natural gifts needed by the philosopher cf. *Republic* 484ff, especially 486D.

3. The same image of friction producing a spark is used in *Republic* 435A where conclusions about justice in the state and justice in the individual are to be 'rubbed together' to produce a spark which will illuminate the real nature of justice.

writer is a serious man, that his book does not represent his most serious thoughts; they remain stored up in the noblest region of his personality. If he is really serious in what he has set down in writing 'then surely' not the gods but men 'have robbed him of his wits'.[1]

Anyone who has followed the account given in this digression will see clearly that if Dionysius or another, small or great, has written anything on the first and highest principles of nature, he cannot to my way of thinking have had any sound knowledge of the subject on which he writes; if he had he would feel the same reverence for truth as I, and would not have dared to expose it to discredit in a world with which it is out of tune. It cannot be that he has written to assist his memory; there is no danger of a man forgetting the truth, once his soul has grasped it, since it lies within a very small compass. No, if he in fact has written at all, it must have been to gratify a base ambition, either by pretending that these thoughts were his own or else by appearing to share a culture of which he was not worthy, since his reason for pursuing it was simply the reputation that would result from its acquisition. If Dionysius acquired this understanding from a single conversation with me, so be it; but how he could have done so Gude kens, as the Theban says,[2] for I went through the matter with him in the way I have described once only; never again. Anyone who is anxious to know about what followed must consider why it was that we did not repeat the lesson a second and third time, or even oftener. Did Dionysius after that single session suppose that he knew enough and did he in fact know enough, either because he had found things out for himself or because he had learnt them earlier from others? Or did he think that what I told him was of no importance? Or, a third possibility, did he realize that my teaching was beyond his capacity, and that he would never be able to live a life devoted to wisdom and virtue? If he thought what I have to say

345

1. A quotation from Homer, *Iliad*, 7.460.
2. cf. *Phaedo* 62A, where the same dialect phrase is used by Cebes, a Theban.

trivial, he will have to encounter testimony to the opposite effect from many who are probably much weightier judges of such a matter than he is. If, on the other hand, he believed that he had discovered or learnt already something which is nevertheless valuable for the education of a free spirit, how, unless he is a most extraordinary person, could he so recklessly have brought dishonour upon the man who is the guide and authority in this matter? That, however, is exactly what he did, as I will now tell you.

PLATO'S LAST DEALINGS WITH DIONYSIUS AND HIS DEPARTURE FROM SYRACUSE

The letter returns to straightforward narrative which requires little comment. It is to be noted, however, that the account given here differs in some points from that given by Plutarch in his life of Dion, in spite of the fact that Plutarch unquestionably regarded the letter as authentic. In speaking of Plato's departure Plutarch explicitly says that his account does not entirely tally with 'Plato's own words', but it is clear that he retains the alternative version in order not to sacrifice a good story. 'You will, no doubt,' he makes Dionysius say to Plato, 'speak very ill of me to your fellow-philosophers.' 'I hope we shall never be so short of matter in the Academy,' replied Plato with a smile, 'as to need to mention you'.

Not long after the events already described Dionysius, who hitherto had allowed Dion to retain his property and enjoy the income from it, forbade Dion's agents to send remittances to the Peloponnese, in apparent utter forgetfulness of what he had said in his letter. He declared that Dion's estate belonged now no longer to Dion but to Dion's son, who was his own nephew and therefore his legal ward. This was the position of affairs at the point that we have reached. When this happened I saw clearly what Dionysius' enthusiasm for philosophy amounted to, and I had good ground for indignation, whether I liked it or not. It was now summer and the sailing season; so I decided that, though I had no more reason to be angry with

Dionysius than with myself and with those who constrained me to come for the third time to the Strait of Scylla, 'once more to retrace my course to the dangers of deadly Charybdis',[1] I ought to tell Dionysius that in view of his shameful treatment of Dion I could stay with him no longer. Dionysius tried to pacify me and begged me to stay, thinking that it would not be well for him that I should depart in a hurry bearing such news in person, but when he could not prevail on me he promised that he would himself arrange transport for me. My intention was to embark on the first ship to set sail, so angry was I, and I was prepared to face anything that might happen to me if I were prevented, since it was perfectly clear that I was the innocent and injured party. But when Dionysius saw that I had not the smallest desire to stay he hit upon the following way of keeping me there for that sailing season. He came next day and put to me this plausible proposal: 'Let us rid ourselves of the disagreements in which Dion and his affairs are always involving us. For your sake this is what I will do for Dion. I am willing to let him receive his property and live in the Peloponnese, not as an exile but with the possibility of returning to Syracuse, when he and I and you who are his friends agree that he should do so. My only condition is that he should not conspire against me; for this you and your friends and Dion's friends here must go bail, and you in turn must get security from him. Whatever funds he receives shall be deposited in the Peloponnese or at Athens with trustees of your choosing; Dion shall enjoy the income, but is not to withdraw the capital without your consent. I do not feel sure that Dion would do the right thing by me if he had his considerable fortune at his disposal, but I have more confidence in you and your friends. See if you find this proposal satisfactory; if you do, stay for this year, and then depart for good taking Dion's property with you. I am sure that Dion will be very grateful to you if you arrange things for him on these terms.'

1. Homer, *Odyssey* 12, 428. These words are quoted as from Plato by Plutarch, *Dion* 18.

I was vexed by this proposal, but I said that I would think about it and give him my decision on the following day. That was what we agreed. When I was alone I debated the matter with myself in great perplexity, but the thought which came uppermost in my mind was this. 'It may be that Dionysius has no intention of keeping any of his promises, but suppose that after my departure he writes a plausible letter to Dion, and gets a number of Dion's friends to do the same, detailing the proposal he has just made to me, and saying that in spite of his offer I refused to play any part in what he suggested and showed myself completely indifferent to Dion's interests. Suppose too that he does not want to let me go, and without giving any actual order lets it be known among the ships' captains, as he easily could, that he is averse from my sailing; would any of them be prepared in those circumstances to take me on board, setting out, as I should have to do, from the house of Dionysius?' (I should say that, to add to my difficulties, I was then living in the palace garden, from which the porter too would have refused to let me out without an express order to that effect from Dionysius.) 'If I stay for this year I shall be able to let Dion know my situation and what I am doing, and if Dionysius keeps his word I shall have achieved something by no means derisory, for at a proper valuation Dion's fortune is probably not less than a hundred talents. If on the other hand the situation develops in the way that seems likely I do not see what I am to do. Nevertheless it would appear that I must stick things out for another year, and put Dionysius' intentions to the test of actual experience.'

Having come to this conclusion I told Dionysius the following day that I had decided to stay. 'But', I added, 'you must not regard me as empowered to act for Dion. We must send him a joint letter embodying the present proposition, and ask if he is satisfied with it. If he is not and wishes to put forward any alternative he should write at once, and you must promise not to take any further action about him in the mean time.' That was what I said, and that was what we agreed in almost these very terms. So the ships sailed, and then, when it was no longer possible for me to go, Dionysius remarked to me that only half the property should go to Dion and the other half to his son. The whole was to be sold, and I should have half the proceeds to take for Dion, while the other half was left in Sicily for his son; that was the fairest thing to do. I was stunned by this remark, and it seemed absurd to say anything more; however, I said that we must wait for Dion's letter and then send him this further proposal. Immediately after this Dionysius in the most wanton way sold the whole of Dion's property, on his own terms and to purchasers of his own choice, without saying a word to me about it. And I for my part refrained from saying anything further to him about Dion's affairs, for I thought that nothing was to be gained by reopening the matter.

This is the story so far of my attempt to come to the aid of philosophy and of my friends, but from that time onward the terms on which Dionysius and I lived were these. I was like a bird looking out from its cage and longing to fly away, while Dionysius was seeking for a way of keeping Dion's property by scaring me off the subject. Nevertheless, before Sicily at large we maintained a façade of friendship. 348

Now Dionysius, contrary to his father's policy, attempted to reduce the pay of his older mercenaries. The troops gathered in an angry mob and refused to acquiesce. Dionysius, in an attempt to compel them, shut the gates of the citadel; whereupon they charged straight at the walls, shouting a war-cry in their own barbaric tongue. At this Dionysius took fright and granted to the assembled soldiery all they demanded and more.

A rumour soon spread that Heracleides[1] was at the bottom of this trouble, and when it reached him he went into hiding. Dionysius, thwarted in his efforts to arrest him, summoned

1. Heracleides held a military command under Dionysius. After his escape he joined Dion in Greece, and returned to Sicily in command of a fleet shortly after Dion's capture of Syracuse. For the story of his subsequent intrigues against Dion, which led ultimately to his own and Dion's death, the chief authority is Plutarch in his life of Dion. Theodotes was the uncle of Heracleides.

Theodotes to his garden, where I also happened to be walking at that time. What other talk passed between them I do not know, for I did not hear it, but I remember distinctly what Theodotes said to Dionysius in my presence. 'Plato,' he said, 'I am trying to persuade our friend Dionysius that if I succeed in bringing Heracleides into his presence to answer what he is now charged with, and if Dionysius decides that Heracleides should no longer dwell in Sicily, he should be allowed to take his wife and son and to live in the Peloponnese, enjoying the income of his property, provided that he does Dionysius no harm. I have already sent for him once and I will send again; it may be that he will respond to one or other of these messages. But I beg and beseech Dionysius that, wherever Heracleides is found, either here or in the country, no penalty shall be inflicted on him beyond banishment abroad during Dionysius' pleasure. Do you agree to that?' he said, turning to Dionysius. 'Yes, I agree,' replied Dionysius; 'even if he is found in your house nothing shall happen to him beyond what you have said.' The following evening Theodotes and Eurybius came running to me in a state of great perturbation. 'Plato,' said Theodotes, 'you were there yesterday when Dionysius made a compact with us both about Heracleides?' 'Indeed I was,' I answered. 'Well now,' he went on, 'troops are scouring the country in pursuit of Heracleides, and it may well be that he is somewhere in this neighbourhood. Come with us to Dionysius without losing a moment.' So we set off and when we got into Dionysius' presence the two of them stood weeping silently, while I said: 'Our friends are afraid that you may be taking some step about Heracleides contrary to yesterday's agreement, for I believe that he has returned and has been seen about here.' At this Dionysius flared up and went all colours, like a man in a rage. Theodotes fell at his feet and, grasping his hand, begged him with tears not to do such a thing, while I by way of comforting him said: 'Take heart, Theodotes; Dionysius will never dare to violate the agreement we made yesterday.' 'I made no agreement of any kind whatever with *you*,' said Dionysius, giving me a very

349

despotic look. 'God knows you did,' said I; 'you promised to refrain from the very course which Theodotes is begging you not to take.' With these words I turned away and left him. After this he continued to hunt for Heracleides, but Theodotes got a message to him urging him to take refuge in flight. Dionysius sent out Tisias and a detachment with orders to pursue him, but Heracleides succeeded in reaching Carthaginian territory a few hours ahead of them.

After this Dionysius concluded that the old plot might furnish a decent pretext for hostile relations with me, so that he need not part with Dion's property. His first step was to remove me from the citadel, on the ground that the garden in which I was then living was needed for a female religious festival which would last ten days; his orders were that I should lodge outside with Archedemus for this period. While I was there Theodotes sent for me and poured out a long and indignant string of complaints about Dionysius' behaviour. Dionysius, hearing that I had visited Theodotes, and using this as a further ground for quarrelling with me, akin to the former, sent to ask me if my visits had taken place at Theodotes' invitation. 'Certainly,' I answered. 'In that case,' said the messenger, 'I was to tell you that you are behaving ill in always preferring Dion and Dion's friends to Dionysius.' That was the message, and after that he never summoned me back to the palace, but took it as established that I was the friend of Theodotes and Heracleides and therefore his enemy; besides, he did not believe in my good-will on account of the utter ruin of Dion's property. So from that time I lived outside the citadel among the mercenaries. 350

Various people now visited me, among them some members of ships' crews who hailed from Athens and were my fellow-countrymen; they reported to me that I had a bad name among the light infantry, who were threatening to kill me if they could lay hands on me. To provide for my safety I sent a message to Archytas and my other friends at Tarentum telling them my situation. They found some pretext for a diplomatic mission from their city and sent Lamiscus, one of their own

PLATO

number, with a thirty-oared vessel. On his arrival he made
representations to Dionysius on my behalf, telling him that I
was anxious to depart, and begging him not to stand in my
way. So Dionysius gave way and sent me off with money for
my journey, but as for Dion's property I neither asked for nor
received any part of it whatever.

When I reached Olympia in the Peloponnese I found Dion
attending the festival and told him what had happened. He
swore that he would have satisfaction, and called upon me and
my relations and friends to prepare to punish Dionysius for
the wrongs he had done, in my case by failure to discharge his
obligations as my host – that was what Dion thought and said
– and in Dion's by an unjust sentence of banishment and
exile. When I heard this I told him that he was welcome to call
upon my friends, if they would listen to him. 'But for my
part,' I said, 'you and the others in a way compelled me to
share Dionysius' hearth and table and to take part with him
in the rites of religion. He probably believed the allegations of
all those who told him that I was conspiring with you against
him and his authority; yet for all that his conscience restrained
him from putting me to death. So, leaving aside the fact that I
am almost past the age to help anyone in war, I am impartially
at the service of you both if ever you wish to be friends and to
benefit one another, but as long as you are set on doing harm
you must look elsewhere.' This I said in disgust at my
Sicilian 'adventures' and their unhappy outcome. But they
would not listen to me or entertain my suggestions of concilia-
tion, and are therefore responsible for all the harm that has
come upon them. If Dionysius had restored Dion's property
or had been completely reconciled with him, in all human
probability none of this would have happened – I could
easily have restrained Dion, for I had both the desire and the
power to do so; but as things are they have attacked one
another and brought about universal ruin.

351   Yet Dion's policy was what I should say that mine or any
reasonable man's should be; as far as his own power and his
friends and his country are concerned such a man will aim to

148

attain supreme authority and honour simply by performing the
greatest public service. I do not call it public service when a
poor man, who is unable to control his passions or resist the
temptations of pleasure, in order to enrich himself and his
party and his city collects a gang of conspirators, and then,
when he has put the wealthy to death as public enemies,
dissipates their property and encourages his accomplices and
followers to do the same, in order that none of them may say
that it is *his* fault that they are poor. Nor do I mean honour
acquired by services which consist in carrying laws to distri-
bute the property of the few among the many or, if the state of
which a man is head is powerful and the mistress of many
smaller states, wrongfully appropriating the possessions of
those smaller states for his own state. Neither Dion nor any
other man would by deliberate choice set out to acquire in this
way a power which would be a curse for ever to himself and
his family; his aim will be the political and legal system that is
fairest and best, and that does not involve sentences of death
or exile in the smallest degree. This was the ideal that Dion
pursued, believing that it is better to be the victim of wickedness than to be its author; but, though he took precautions to
protect himself, he tripped nevertheless at the very moment
when his triumph over his enemies was complete. We need
feel no surprise at this. In dealing with the wicked a good man
of sense and discretion is not likely to be wholly at fault about
their nature; yet he may very well suffer the fate of a good
seaman, who knows well enough that a storm is coming, but
may be taken unawares by its sudden and exceptional violence,
and in consequence overwhelmed. This was what undid Dion.
He knew that those who brought about his destruction were
thoroughly bad men; what he did not realize was the depth of
their ignorance and wickedness and greed. To this he fell a
victim, and brought upon Sicily infinite grief.

The advice I have to give in the situation that has arisen
since his death has mostly been given already; so let that
suffice. I have gone back over the story of my second visit to
Sicily because it seemed to me that the strange and improbable

352

nature of the events made such an account necessary. If anyone finds that what I have said makes those events more intelligible, and understands that in the circumstances I have described there were sufficient reasons for what happened, this account will have accomplished adequately what it set out to do.

THE EIGHTH LETTER

*

The Eighth Letter presupposes a different situation in Sicily from that of the Seventh. Some time has elapsed since the murder of Dion, and his adherents have formed common cause with Hipparinus, son of Dionysius I and half-brother of Dionysius II, who expelled Callippus from Syracuse in 352 after a tyranny of thirteen months, and was himself killed in a drunken quarrel two years later. Since the letter (356A) speaks of Hipparinus' upright character, it must belong to the early days of his rule, or even to the period before the expulsion of Callippus. It is clear also that Dionysius II, though he no longer has a foothold in Syracuse, has by no means given up the struggle to regain his power.

It is to be noted that the letter speaks of the proposals for concilia-tion which it contains as being little more than a pious hope. Yet even so it seems curious that Plato should think that the advice which he offers had even a remote chance of being adopted. What was going on in Sicily was a naked and ruthless struggle for power, and the kind of compromise between Dionysius and the other factions which the letter suggests was quite incapable of surviving even if it could have been momentarily achieved. If the Eighth Letter was written by Plato, it has to be admitted that it does little credit to his judgement of political realities.

The letter also contains a serious historical difficulty. It proposes the establishment of a mixed constitution under three kings, whose power is to be subject to much the same checks and limitations as that of the kings of Sparta. The three kings are to be Dionysius himself, his half-brother Hipparinus, with whom Dion's party is in alliance, and an unnamed son of Dion. Two sons of Dion are known, one, also called Hipparinus, who is said by Plutarch to have died in early man-hood before his father (cf. Letter VII n. 1), the other a posthumous child born in prison after Dion's death. Some hold that it is the second who is in question here, and that it is natural that being an infant he should be unnamed. This seems inconsistent with the state-ment at 357C that Plato's plan exists in two minds 'the minds of

Hipparinus, son of Dionysius and of my own (i. e. Dion's) son'.
Alternatively, it has been suggested that Plato did not know of the
death of Dion's elder son, or even that the statement that he died
before his father is untrue. None of these hypotheses seems satisfactory,
and the difficulty, which has been urged as an argument against the
authenticity of the letter, must be left unresolved.

PLATO TO THE RELATIONS AND FRIENDS OF DION, GREETINGS

I will endeavour to make as clear to you as I can the policy
which you will find most conducive to your true welfare. The
advice which I have to offer is meant not only for you,
though it is you of course that I have primarily in mind; it is
addressed in the second place to the whole body of Syracusans,
and in the third even to your opponents and enemies, except-
ing only the criminal:[1] their actions are irreparable and can
never be blotted out. Attend now to what I say.

Since the overthrow of the tyranny, you have had throughout the whole of Sicily nothing but strife on this single point:
one party wishes to recover its power, the other to make its
escape from tyranny final and permanent. In such circumstances the policy which always recommends itself to most
people is that which will do most harm to their enemies and
good to their friends. It is however by no means easy to inflict
great injury on others without at the same time bringing great
harm upon oneself. You do not have to go far afield to see the
truth of this; just consider what has happened here in Sicily,
where one side is trying to inflict damage and the other to
protect itself against it, a story which you might pass on to
others to their great profit, though there is no lack of examples
to illustrate this lesson. But a policy which will benefit
enemies and friends alike, or at any rate cause least harm to
both sides, is not easy to devise or to put into effect when one
has devised it; to give such advice and attempt to amplify it

1. This presumably refers to Callippus, and may imply that he has not
yet been expelled from Syracuse.

seems little but a pious hope. Let it be a pious hope by all means – any attempt to speak or think should begin with an appeal to the gods – and may it find fulfilment when it speaks to us somewhat as follows.

You and your enemies, ever since the war began,[1] have been ruled almost continuously by a single family. Your fathers put it in power at a time of grave emergency, when there was a danger that the whole of Greek Sicily would be overrun by the Carthaginians and fall completely into barbarian hands. Then it was that they chose Dionysius, a young and energetic soldier, to conduct the operations of war for which he was well fitted, and associated with him as his adviser Hipparinus, an older man, giving them, to save Sicily, the position of 'commanders[2] with absolute power'. Now whether it was the divine providence of God or the valour of the commanders or a combination of both supported by the citizens of that time that brought deliverance makes no matter; ascribe it to what you will; at any rate safety was assured for that generation. It was no doubt right and proper that all should be grateful to their deliverers for the qualities they had displayed, but if subsequently the absolute rulers have abused the gift which the city bestowed on them, they have in part paid the penalty for this already, and should not escape payment of what is outstanding. What then, we must ask, is the penalty which would inevitably be right in their present circumstances?

If you could escape from their clutches easily and without great risk and trouble, or if they were able without difficulty to recover their power, there would be no point in giving you the advice that I am about to give. As it is, however, both sides should call to mind and consider how often each has confidently believed that it needed but a trifle to achieve complete success, and how this trifle has on each occasion turned out to be the cause of disasters beyond counting. The limit is never reached; what seems to be an end merges again

1. The war is war against Carthage, which had been intermittently carried on since the closing years of the fifth century.
2. Reading στρατηγούς for τυράννους.

and again into a new beginning, and it looks as if this vicious cycle will result in the destruction of absolutists and democrats alike. The probable outcome, which God forbid, will be that the Greek language will practically cease to be spoken over the whole of Sicily, and that the island will fall into the hands of some Phoenician or Oscan power.[1] This is a situation for which every Greek should do all in his power to find a remedy. If anyone has a better or more effective remedy than what I am going to suggest, let him bring it forward and earn in its truest sense the title of 'friend of Greece'.

354

What seems to me the best course I will try to make clear with complete frankness and without partiality to either side. I am in the position of an arbitrator between two parties, one the former possessor and the other the former subject of absolute power, and my advice, which is not new, is addressed to each party separately. To any absolute ruler my advice would be to avoid both the name and the reality of absolute power, and to turn it, if possible, into kingship. That such a course is possible is demonstrated by the example of the wise and good Lycurgus,[2] who saw that members of his own family in Argos and Messene had transformed themselves from kings into absolute rulers and thereby destroyed both themselves and their respective states. Fearing therefore for his own state as well as for his family he found a remedy by giving authority to the elders and by making the ephors a salutary check upon the power of the kings. In this way the state has been gloriously preserved for all the generations since his time, since law became the sovereign king over men instead of men becoming arbitrary masters of the law.

1. Carthage was in origin Phoenician. The Oscans are people of central Italy from whom, among others, Dionysius had recruited mercenaries. When Timoleon arrived in 344 B.C. they were in occupation of several Sicilian cities.

2. Lycurgus was the traditional founder of the Spartan constitution, in which a council of elders and five annually elected *ephors* constituted a powerful check on the two hereditary kings. It is to be noted that the word 'king' (*basileus*) conveys in Greek no suggestion of autocracy; the word for a despot or dictator is 'tyrant' (*turannos*).

This is what I recommend now, as he did then. I urge those who are grasping at absolute power to turn away and run with all their might from what fools who are insatiably greedy call happiness, and to try to transform themselves into the shape of kings and to obey the laws which govern that office, secure in the possession of honour both from willing subjects and from the law. Similarly I would urge those whose aim is a free way of life and to whom the yoke of slavery is an evil they would shun to be on their guard lest through an excessive and unseasonable eagerness for liberty they succumb to the disease which afflicted their ancestors, when in their boundless desire for freedom they experienced the evils of anarchy carried to the extreme. Before the reigns of Dionysius and Hipparinus the Sicilians were living what they thought a happy life, in the enjoyment of luxury and at the same time of control over their rulers; they even stoned to death without any legal trial the ten commanders who preceded Dionysius,[1] in order that they should be subject to no master, however righteous and lawful his authority, but be absolutely free. That is how they got their tyrants. Servitude and liberty when they run to excess are both utterly bad, but in proper measure either is a very great blessing. To be the servant of God is the proper measure of servitude; excess consists in being the servant of men. And the god of wise men is the law, whereas fools make pleasure their god.

355

Since this is so, I urge the friends of Dion to communicate what I have to say to all the Syracusans as the joint advice of Dion and myself; I will interpret to you what he would say himself if he were alive and able to speak to you now. You may ask, 'What message relevant to our present situation can we derive from Dion's advice?' The message is this.

'First of all, men of Syracuse, give your adherence to laws which it is plain will not turn your thoughts towards money-making and wealth. Soul, body, and wealth are three separate

1. Diodorus Siculus states that after the fall of Acragas to the Carthaginians in 406 the Syracusans deposed their generals and chose others, one of them Dionysius I, but does not mention the stoning.

things; range them in an order in which the highest honour is paid to excellence of soul, and the third and lowest to wealth, which should be the servant of body and soul alike.[1] The ordinance which produces this effect you would do well to adopt as an established law, since it results in the real happiness of those who observe it; the kind of reasoning which calls the rich happy is wretched in itself, being merely the foolish talk of women and children, and makes those who follow it wretched. The truth of what I say you can verify by experience, if you are prepared to make trial of what I am now saying about laws. Experience is the truest touchstone of any matter.

'Once you have adopted such laws, at a moment when Sicily is in peril and you are neither in adequate control yourselves nor decisively under the control of others, the right and expedient course for you all will be to make a compromise. On the one side are those who wish to escape the harshness of absolute rule, on the other those who passionately long to regain their power. It was their ancestors, remember, who performed the supreme service of saving the Greeks from the barbarians, and made it possible for you now to be debating a form of constitution; if they had then come to ruin there would be no debate now and no hope remaining whatsoever. So, as things are, let one side obtain liberty under the rule of kings, and the other the power of kings subject to the law, and let the law be master not only of the citizens in general but of the kings themselves, if they transgress it. With God's help then and with a sincere and honest intention to fulfil all these conditions appoint three kings. Let the first be my son,[2] because of the double debt you owe to me and to my father; he freed the state from barbarians in time past, and I, as you have seen for yourselves, have twice delivered it from absolute rulers.[3] In the second place appoint as king my father's namesake, who is the son of Dionysius, in recognition of the help

356

1. For the same classification cf. *Laws* 697B, 743E.
2. Hipparinus, cf. introductory note.
3. cf. Letter VII 333B (p. 125 above).

he has recently given you and of his upright character; though he is the son of a tyrant he is lending his willing aid to liberate the city, and by doing so is acquiring for himself and his family eternal honour in exchange for the ephemeral advantage of an unrighteous rule. Third, you must invite to become king of Syracuse – and the offer and its acceptance must be equally ungrudging – the man who is at present at the head of the host of your enemies, Dionysius, the son of Dionysius. It may be that he will be ready to exchange his present position for a kingship, partly from fear of what fate has in store and partly from pity for his country with its neglected temples and tombs; persistence in his ambition may involve total ruin and expose him to the triumph of the barbarians.

'These three kings, whether you confer on them the powers of the kings at Sparta or agree upon a diminution of their authority, you should constitute in the following way. This has already been expounded to you, but hear it yet once more. If the family of Dionysius and Hipparinus is willing for the salvation of Sicily to put an end to the present troubles and to accept an honourable position for themselves now and for their descendants hereafter, on these conditions, as I have said, invite them to send plenipotentiaries to arrange a settlement; the selection and number of the representatives should be left to them, and they may be natives of Sicily or foreigners or a mixture of both. When they arrive let them first promulgate laws and a constitution of a type that leaves the kings in control of the rites of religion and of such other matters as it is proper to entrust to former benefactors, while the power of war and peace is in the hands of thirty-five 'guardians of the law' acting in concert with a popular assembly and a council. Other courts can deal with minor matters, but the power to inflict death or banishment must belong to the 'guardians of the law', with whom must be associated judges selected annually from among the officials of the previous year, one with the highest reputation for upright conduct from each class of officials. These shall be the judges for the ensuing year in any case which involves the

death or imprisonment or banishment of a citizen. A king shall
not be eligible to act as judge in such cases; he must keep
himself clear, like a priest, from pollution by bloodshed or
imprisonment or exile.[1]

'These were the intentions which I had for you while I was
alive and they are my intentions still. When with your help I
had overcome our enemies I should, if I had not been
prevented by fiends in the guise of friends,[2] have put these
plans into effect. Next, if the effect corresponded with my
intention, I should have settled the rest of Sicily, taking from
the barbarians the territory which they now hold, except for
those who fought to the end against the tyrant for our common freedom, and restoring the original inhabitants of the
Greek regions to the homes of their fathers. These same
plans I now urge you to adopt and to put into effect as your
joint policy, inviting the cooperation of all and regarding any
man who refuses it as your common enemy. What I suggest is
really not impossible. A plan which exists in two minds and
which any reflective person can readily discover to be the best
can hardly be dismissed as impossible without folly. When I
say 'two minds' I mean the minds of Hipparinus, son of
Dionysius and of my own son; I suppose that all Syracusans
who have the interest of the state at heart would fall in with
whatever these two have agreed upon. So offer honour and
prayers to the gods, and to all whom it is proper to associate
with the gods; employ persuasion and gentle encouragement
upon friends and adversaries alike, and above all do not give
up until you have brought these plans, which as I describe
them, are but waking dreams sent by the gods, to successful
and visible realization before the eyes of men.'

1. The mixed constitution sketched here has much in common with
that suggested by Plato for his Cretan city in the *Laws*. cf. especially
Laws 752ff, where the election and functions of a body of 'guardians of
the law' of similar size are described in detail. In particular both contain
the provision that in the supreme court for capital cases ex-magistrates
shall be associated with the 'guardians of the law' (*Laws* 855c).
2. Dion's murderers, Callippus and Philostratus; cf. Letter VII 333cff.

SELECT BIBLIOGRAPHY

*

PHAEDRUS

DE VRIES, G. J., *A Commentary on the Phaedrus of Plato*, Amsterdam, 1969.

HACKFORTH, R., *Plato's Phaedrus* (translation and commentary), 1952 (reprinted in Library of Liberal Arts, Indianapolis).

THOMPSON, W. H., *The Phaedrus of Plato* (text and commentary), 1868.

*

HAMILTON, W., Plato, *Gorgias*, Penguin Classics, 1960.

HAMILTON, W., Plato, *Symposium*, Penguin Classics, 1951.

LEE, H. D. P., Plato, *Republic*, Penguin Classics, 1955.

SAUNDERS, A. N. W., *Greek Political Oratory*, Penguin Classics, 1970.

*

RAVEN, J. E., *Plato's Thought in the Making*, 1965.

SHOREY, P., *What Plato Said*, Chicago, 1933 (abridged edn 1965).

TAYLOR. A. E., *Plato, the Man and his Work* (7th edn reprinted), 1966.

PLATONIC LETTERS

HARWARD, J., *The Platonic Epistles* (translation and commentary), 1932.

MORROW, G. R., *Plato's Epistles* (translation and critical essays), Library of Liberal Arts, Indianapolis, 1962.

POST, L. A., *Thirteen Epistles of Plato* (translation and notes), 1925.

*

SAUNDERS, T. J., Plato, *The Laws*, Penguin Classics, 1970.

*

FIELD, G. C., *Plato and his Contemporaries*, 3rd edn 1967.

FINLEY, M. I., *Plato and Practical Politics* in *Aspects of Antiquity*, 1968.
Mary Renault's novel *The Mask of Apollo* (1966) contains an interesting imaginative reconstruction, based mainly on the Seventh Letter, of Plato's experiences in Sicily.